BOSTON TERRIER

PATRICIA F. LEHMAN

Boston Terrier

Project Team
Editor: Stephanie Fornino
Copy Editor: Joann Woy
Indexer: Lucie Haskins
Designer: Mike Bencze
Series Designer: Mary Ann Kahn

TFH Publications®
President/CEO: Glen S. Axelrod
Executive Vice President: Mark E. Johnson
Editor-in-Chief: Albert Connelly, Jr.
Production Manager: Kathy Bontz

TFH Publications, Inc.®
One TFH Plaza
Third and Union Avenues
Neptune City, NJ 07753

Printed and bound in China

14 15 16 17 18 19   1 3 5 7 9 8 6 4 2

Library of Congress Cataloging-in-Publication Data

Lehman, Patricia F., 1955-
  Boston terrier / Patricia F. Lehman.
    p. cm.
  Includes index.
  ISBN 978-0-7938-3732-8 (alk. paper)
  1. Boston terrier. I. Title.
  SF429.B7L44 2012
  636.72--dc23

2011041969

This book has been published with the intent to provide accurate and authoritative information in regard to the subject matter within. While every reasonable precaution has been taken in preparation of this book, the author and publisher expressly disclaim responsibility for any errors, omissions, or adverse effects arising from the use or application of the information contained herein. The techniques and suggestions are used at the reader's discretion and are not to be considered a substitute for veterinary care. If you suspect a medical problem consult your veterinarian.

Note: In the interest of concise writing, "he" is used when referring to puppies and dogs unless the text is specifically referring to females or males. "She" is used when referring to people. However, the information contained herein is equally applicable to both sexes.

The Leader In Responsible Animal Care for Over 50 Years!®
www.tfh.com

CONTENTS

ORIGINS OF YOUR
BOSTON TERRIER

F rom the tree-lined, cobblestone streets of Beacon
   Hill, in Boston, Massachusetts, comes a small but
   sporty dog who has captivated fanciers with his
dapper appearance and charming personality. Weighing
less than 25 pounds (11.5 kg), he is sturdy and compact,
yet graceful and well balanced. His short, easy-care
coat—which may be brindle, seal, or black, accented
by distinctive white tuxedo markings—enhances his
dynamic, clean-cut appearance.

The Boston Terrier is an ideal family pet. Playful with
children while equally fond of senior citizens, he is an
indoor breed who thrives on the companionship of
his human family. The Boston Terrier is an intelligent,
trainable, and eager-to-please breed whose tidy habits
and good manners have earned him the nickname
"American Gentleman."

AN AMERICAN ORIGINAL

As the fog lifted off England's River Mersey in 1865, a
well-built, dark-brindle-and-white canine waited on

The Boston Terrier
is an intelligent,
trainable, and eager-
to-please breed whose
tidy habits and good
manners have earned
him the nickname
"American Gentleman."

the bustling Liverpool dock to board the steamship bound for America. After
a fortnight at sea, he was released to William O'Brien, who sold him in 1870 to
Robert C. Hooper. Little could the dog—now called Hooper's Judge—foresee
his destiny as the founder of the first breed developed solely within the United
States. Judge was a cross between a Bulldog and a Bull or English Terrier, said to
possess the best qualities of each. At home on the Hooper estate, Judge was
soon picked by fellow Bostonian Edward Burnett to sire a litter by his small, white
female, named Burnett's Gyp. The result was Well's Eph, a strong, low-stationed,
dark-brindle male.

From the mating of Eph with golden-brindle Tobin's Kate came a pair of
brothers, Barnard's Tom and Atkinson's Toby. With his red-brindle coat and white
forehead, collar, chest, and feet, Tom was "the first to show that fine quality that
is present in a good specimen of the modern Boston Terrier," said J. Varnum Mott,
MD, in his 1906 book, *The Boston Terrier*. Tom and Toby were used extensively
at stud, with much inbreeding of the best sons and daughters. However, several
small imported dogs were also brought in to introduce fresh blood into the
original line. One of Tom's sons—the pick of the litter, named Barnard's Mike—was
a light brindle and the first to have the full, round eyes so favored in the breed.

Chosen by John P. Barnard in lieu of Tom's stud fee, Mike not only was deemed the first true Boston Terrier but also passed on his fine qualities to his many offspring. Four other dogs played key roles in the breed's development: Goode's Buster, Bixby's Tony Boy, Sullivan's Punch, and Cracksman. Each contributed his merits—color, size, and temperament—to form distinctive strains that stand behind many of today's pedigrees.

FOUNDING FATHERS: HOOPER AND BURNETT

As a seventh-generation descendant of William W. Hooper, who set sail on the *James* in 1635 for a two-month voyage from London to the New World, Robert Chamblet Hooper was born in 1849 into one of Boston's oldest and wealthiest families. For three generations, the Hoopers made their fortunes at sea—building and selling ships, and importing goods for sale on the Central and Constitution Wharves. Robert grew up with his five siblings at Oakland, a newly built "Italianate, cupola-topped mansion," on 20 acres in the heart of Dorchester. He entered Harvard University but left in his junior year—as did his own father—to sail around the world. At 21, he acquired the dog who would launch the Boston Terrier breed.

The Boston has captivated fanciers with his dapper appearance and charming personality.

Whether Hooper continued to participate in the sport of dogs is unknown, but he achieved renown in steeplechase circles, racing under the name "Mr. Chamblet." He served as Steward of the National Steeplechase and Hunt Association and won several Grand National races on New York courses. Robert C. Hooper died at age 60, leaving his teenage daughter as his only survivor.

Edward Burnett grew up in a stone mansion built by his father, Joseph, on land acquired for the family's Deerfoot Farm, a successful dairy and sausage venture. The Burnett family's patriarch had also settled in Massachusetts in the late 1630s. From modest beginnings as rope makers and small farmers, Joseph grew the family fortune by developing and selling flavorings, such as vanilla extract, at Joseph Burnett & Company, near Central Wharf. The eldest of 12 children, Edward was a student at Harvard—possibly with Hooper—when the seminal breeding of Judge and Gyp took place. It's said that Burnett owned as many as 13 Bostons, who used to accompany him on his farm duties and eagerly dispatch any vermin that dared show themselves. In later years, Burnett served as a Representative to the Fiftieth Congress (1887 to 1889), and Deerfoot became the New England headquarters for Grover Cleveland's 1892 presidential campaign. Following his brief foray into politics, Burnett utilized his degree in architecture to design barns for the cattle he imported for gentlemen farmers, including George W. Vanderbilt, at Biltmore Farms in North Carolina.

The Boston thrives on the companionship of his human family.

ESTABLISHING A CLUB

Four years after the first dog show in the United States took place on an Illinois field and six years before the establishment of the American Kennel Club (AKC), the Beantown canine known as the American Bull Terrier, Boston Bulldog, or Round-Headed Bull Terrier stepped its collective paw in the ring at an 1878 show held by the Massachusetts Kennel Club. There, he shared billing with his Bull Terrier cousins. A decade later, when the New England Kennel Club hosted its annual event in Boston, the breed competed under dog-judge Barnard ("the father of the breed") in a special category for "Round-Headed Bull Terriers, any color."

In 1890, with nearly 40 fanciers then in the Boston area, Harvard student Charles F. Leland invited the men to form the American Bull Terrier Club. "Their main object in coming together was not to have a social good time (although, happily, this generally took place), but to further the interests of the dog in every legitimate way," said Edward Axtell in *The Boston Terrier and All About It*.

The first order of business was to draft a blueprint that would accurately delineate the characteristics that distinguished Boston's nascent variety from its crossbred predecessors. As you might imagine, this process didn't sit well with club members, who each thought his own dog represented the ideal type. Some preferred the stocky, low-slung Bulldog, whereas others favored the leaner, sportier terrier. Should the standard conform to the dog—or the dog to the standard? Fortunately, the committee in charge carefully weighed each point to set a breed standard that has changed little in more than a century.

AKC RECOGNITION

The following year, with officers duly elected and the standard in hand, the club applied for membership in the AKC and registration in its Stud Book. Although its application was initially denied because the dog was neither an established breed nor consistent with its original type, its members persevered. They improved their strain, added classes at shows, and established a stud registry with an initial entry of 75 dogs whose pedigrees could be traced back at least three generations.

Perhaps the greatest controversy, however, was the breed's name. Some wanted Round Head, whereas others preferred American Bull Terrier. Both raised the hackles of Bulldog and Bull Terrier enthusiasts, who claimed this upstart bore little resemblance to their own blue-blooded canines. The ultimate chosen name, Boston Terrier, is credited both to Mr. H.W. Lacy, who wrote in an article in the *American Kennel Gazette*, "There is no more interesting story in all dogdom than that of the development of the Boston Terrier," and to James Watson, an AKC founder and head of its Stud Book Committee, who suggested the name to the club's officers.

Because the AKC was less than a decade old, it had never had to contend with embracing a new breed. "But all the time the ancestors of our little dogs of today wagged their tails, wiggled their bodies, and bred true to type, with remarkable consistency for a new breed, and made friends for themselves everywhere," recalled Vincent G. Perry, in his 1928 book, *The Boston Terrier*. The AKC eventually was convinced of the dog's merits, and in 1893 admitted the renamed Boston Terrier Club to its fold. It became the first distinctly made-in-America breed when Hector,

The breed was known by a variety of names, including "Round Head" and "American Bull Terrier," before the name "Boston Terrier" was chosen.

sired by Franklin G. Bixby's Tony Boy, was the first of seven dogs registered that year in the Stud Book.

MAN'S DOG OR LADY'S PET?

Is the Boston Terrier a man's dog or a lady's pet? Whereas early specimens sported the stocky build of the old bull-and-terrier crosses, smaller Bostons frequently took the ribbons in the show ring. By 1906, Watson observed that advocates of the original form made "no use of the dog in any way except as a house pet. To come down to the hard-pan truth the dog was originally a pit terrier. That was his only vocation as a man's dog, and it would be impossible to find one man in the club who would now make use of him in that way. That day is past entirely, and the only thing to consider is the future of the dog." Concessions to both sides resulted in three divisions—lightweight, middleweight, and heavyweight—spanning a minimum of 12 and a maximum of 28 pounds (5.5 and 12.5 kg). The Boston currently competes in one of three categories: under 15 pounds (7 kg), 15 pounds and under 20 pounds (7 and 9 kg), or 20 pounds and not more than 25 pounds (9 and 11.5 kg).

THE BOSTON TERRIER CLUB OF AMERICA (BTCA)

Founded in 1890, the Boston Terrier Club of America (BTCA) started as a group of men and women devoted to the breed and willing to do anything for its advancement. It held monthly meetings on a variety of relevant topics and hosted an annual Specialty Show. The club's main object—

The Boston Terrier Club of America (BTCA) was founded in 1890 by a group of men and women determined to advance the breed.

then as now—was to "promote and encourage the breeding and improvement of the Boston Terrier Dog, as defined by its standard." Today, the BTCA has grown to more than 500 members—breeders, exhibitors, trainers, and pet owners—who participate in dog shows, obedience, agility, and other fun activities with their Bostons. It offers referral assistance for those looking for puppies, as well as rescue services that foster and place dogs for adoption. One of the most important goals is to improve the health of the Boston by encouraging responsible breeding practices and educating members on the latest advances in genetics and veterinary medicine. It also serves as the parent organization to 30-plus affiliate clubs. Its premier public event remains its National Specialty Show—the largest gathering of Boston Terriers in the country—held each spring in different locations.

To learn more about the BTCA or to apply for membership, log onto its website at www.bostonterrierclubofamerica.org.

IN THE SHOW RING

With the establishment of the parent club and acceptance into the AKC Stud Book, the breed was no longer consigned to classes for Bull Terriers or Round-Headed Bull Terriers but took its rightful place in its own division—and later as a member of the Non-Sporting Group—where it competes today. The first champion of record was a granddaughter of Barnard's Mike, named Topsy, who earned her winning points at the 1896 Philadelphia Dog Show. Another who ruled the ring with 75 first-place and special prizes was Champion Monte, sired by Goode's Buster, and said to be "perhaps the greatest show dog of his breed that ever lived."

As the 20th century dawned, the Boston Terrier dominated shows in the Northeast, with more than 100 filling many classes. It was "without doubt the largest supporter of the bench shows of the country and at nine out of ten of them he is in the very marked majority," wrote Mott. "If this may be taken as a criterion of popularity, the breed is the rage of the day."

Unlike British sporting hounds and terriers, which were often imported as finished champions and campaigned by professional handlers, this little fellow brought success to large operations and "kitchen kennels" (small-scale, home-based breeding programs) alike. Among the most successful kennels were Globe (Vincent G. Perry), Mosholu (Madeline C. McGlone), Myrtle Street (John P. Barnard), Presto (J. Varnum Mott, MD), Ravenroyd (Alva Rosenberg), St. Botolph (Edward Axtell), and Trimount (Dr. C.F. Sullivan).

Today, the Boston Terrier competes in the American Kennel Club's (AKC) Non-Sporting Group.

WESTMINSTER KENNEL CLUB NON-SPORTING GROUP WINNERS

Founded in 1877 by a group of sportsmen who gathered to boast of their field exploits at the Westminster Hotel in New York City, the namesake Westminster Kennel Club hosted its First Annual New York Bench Show of Dogs at Gilmore's Garden, an uncovered venue later renamed Madison Square Garden. America's Dog Show, as its annual two-day competition is known, is the country's second-oldest sporting event, with only the Kentucky Derby a year older. The Boston Terrier first pranced into the ring in 1895, and between 1925 and 1987, he won the Non-Sporting Group 8 times and placed an additional 19. This popular showman has never captured the coveted Best in Show trophy, but each February, handlers from all over present worthy contenders at the Garden.

GROUP WINNERS

Group winners over the years include the following:

- 1925: Million Dollar King, owned by Emma G. Fox
- 1929: Ch. Reign Count, owned by Mrs. L.B. Daley
- 1932: Ch. Million Dollar Kid Boots, owned by Mrs. Jesse Thornton
- 1931: Imogene V, owned by William Cornbill
- 1946: Ch. Emperor's Ace, owned by Fred H. Lucas
- 1947 and 1948: Ch. Mighty Sweet Regardless, owned by Claude J. Fitzgerald
- 1970: Ch. Star Q's Brass Buttons, owned by Dr. K. Eileen Hite

For nearly 50 years, the Boston Terrier has consistently reigned among the 20 most popular breeds in America.

A POPULAR BREED

Between 1905 and 1939, when the AKC compiled its statistics at five-year intervals, the Boston regularly ranked first or second in annual registrations. It remained among the top ten through 1963—the only breed to hold that distinction. For nearly 50 years, it has consistently reigned among the 20 most popular breeds in America.

WAR HERO SERGEANT STUBBY

He served his country for 18 months, survived 17 battles, overcame gas and grenade attacks, and captured a German spy. No wonder Sergeant Stubby is a war hero.

BASIC TRAINING

This tale begins in 1917, when local National Guard troops arrived on the campus of Yale University for combat training prior to their deployment with the 102nd Infantry Regiment of the 26th Yankee Division. One day during drills, a small brindle-patched puppy of unknown lineage—said to be a Boston Bull Terrier or part Boston and part pit bull—wandered into their encampment. Befriended by John Robert Conroy and named Stubby for his short tail, the puppy not only practiced bugle calls and drills but also learned to salute by placing his right paw alongside his right eyebrow. Stubby was a great morale booster for these young men who were away from home for the first time and was therefore allowed to remain in camp as the group's mascot.

By the time training ended and the men prepared to embark the USS *Minnesota* bound for France, most had grown so fond of Stubby that they were unwilling to leave him behind. Smuggled aboard under an overcoat, Stubby took shelter in a coal bin until the ship was far enough at sea to safely join his division on deck. Not one to stay inconspicuous, he was soon discovered by the commanding officer. Stubby—recalling his training—executed a proper salute and was allowed to continue his voyage. Even the sailors fell for his charms, with a machinist's mate making him his own dog tag to match those worn by his fellow soldiers.

IN THE TRENCHES

By February 1918, the 26th Yankee Division had arrived on the front lines at Chemin des Dames, where Stubby spent his first month adjusting to life in the trenches amid round-the-clock gunfire. A more sinister threat was the frequent poison gas attacks launched by the German army. A victim himself, Stubby became so attuned to the odor that he is credited with saving his entire company during an early morning raid by running through the trench barking and biting to wake the sleeping men. He vacated the trench and refused to return until the threat had passed.

The Boston's compact stature and outgoing personality make him a versatile breed.

Two months later, Stubby earned his "wound stripe" as his regiment fought to regain the town of Seicheprey from German hands. In a battle that left more than 650 Americans dead or injured, the brave canine sustained wounds to his chest and foreleg from an exploding grenade. Following surgery, during the six weeks he spent recuperating at a Red Cross Recovery Hospital, Stubby roamed the wards to visit other bedridden soldiers before he rejoined his unit on the battlefield.

One of his most important duties was to patrol "no man's land," the region between the trenches of opposing armies, for men who were lost or wounded. Listening for the sounds of the English language and then snaking his way through tangles of barbed wire,

Stubby would track the men and bark for medics or lead the able-bodied back to their trenches. One day, the dog heard noises coming from nearby brush. A man called out, but instead of rescuing the soldier, Stubby flattened his ears and began to bark. The man fled—dog in hot pursuit—fending off bites as he fell to the ground. Stubby summoned the tenacity of his Bulldog kin to hold onto the intruder's breeches until help arrived. The soldiers cheered—Stubby had captured a German spy who had been mapping the positions of Allied trenches! For this, the commander of the 102nd raised Stubby's rank to non-commissioned officer, making him the only dog to be promoted to sergeant through combat. He now outranked his pal, Corporal Conroy.

WAR HERO

Stubby mustered out of wartime service in much the same manner as he mustered in. However, he now donned a handmade chamois coat, embroidered with his name and the flags of the Allied nations, presented to him by women from Chateau-Thierry, grateful to American forces who aided the French in freeing the town from German occupation. On it were displayed his Victory medal and crossbars for the major engagements in which he assisted, alongside numerous medals, pins, and buttons. He was also given an elaborate leather harness with his gold service and wound chevrons attached to the appropriate sides. Legend has it that, at one time, he wore the Iron Cross he had confiscated from his German prisoner.

As the most decorated war dog to date, Sergeant Stubby returned from the Great War to a hero's welcome. He met three presidents, marched in parades, and became an honorary member of the American Legion, Red Cross, and YMCA, where his membership card entitled him to "three bones a day and a place to sleep" for the rest of his life. In 1921, he received a solid-gold medal engraved with his name, commissioned by the Humane Education Society, which was presented personally by General John Joseph "Black Jack" Pershing, Commander-in-Chief of the American Forces in Europe. A newspaper article reported that Stubby "made no reply . . . he merely licked his chops and wagged his diminutive tail."

Following his stint in the military, Conroy enrolled at Georgetown Law, where his faithful companion became the Hoyas' team mascot. Given the football at halftime, Stubby entertained spectators by nudging the ball around the field and is credited with inspiring halftime shows across the country.

After nine years with his master, in 1926, Stubby died in Conroy's arms. His obituary in the *New York Times* ran three columns wide by a half-page long. Wearing the jacket bearing his medals, Stubby's remains are on display in the Smithsonian's *The Price of Freedom: Americans at War* exhibit in Washington, DC.

Gone but not forgotten, Sergeant Stubby also lives on in cyberspace with his own Facebook page "liked" by hundreds of supporters.

INTERESTING FACTS

The following are some fascinating facts about the Boston Terrier.

COLLEGE MASCOTS

Boston University's Terriers athletic teams have been cheered on since 1922 by a costumed Boston Terrier mascot, later called Rhett after the character in *Gone With the Wind*.

Wofford College's Terriers feature the costumed mascot, Boss the Terrier, and his canine partner, Blitz.

POSTAGE STAMPS

The Boston has been a favorite of writers, artists, and intellectuals.

The AKC celebrated its 100th Anniversary in 1984 with a block of postage stamps that recognized five dog-show groups. Designed by Roy Andersen, the Beagle (Hound Group) and Boston Terrier (Non-Sporting Group) shared one of the four stamps.

In 2010, a Boston Terrier named Jake was photographed by Sally Anderson-Bruce for the US Postal Service's "Animal Rescue: Adopt a Shelter Pet" commemorative set.

PRESIDENTIAL PETS

Warren G. Harding owned a Boston Terrier named Hub, and Gerald R. Ford grew up with two Bostons, Fleck and Spot.

BREED RECOGNITION

The first edition of *The American Kennel Gazette and Stud Book* to feature a purebred dog on its cover appeared in 1924, with Carl Anderson's portrait of a Boston Terrier, titled *An American Gentleman*.

The Boston Terrier was chosen in 1976 as the Bicentennial Dog of the United States.

Governor Edward King, who had a childhood Boston Terrier named Skippy, designated the breed the Official State Dog of Massachusetts in 1979.

CHAPTER 2

CHARACTERISTICS OF YOUR BOSTON TERRIER

The Boston's head, which forms a square, rests atop a gracefully arched neck set neatly into sloping shoulders.

How would you describe the ideal Boston Terrier? What traits make him unique? Those were the questions posed by Charles F. Leland and the founding members of the original Boston Terrier Club as they discussed and debated which characteristics from the Bulldog and Bull Terrier should be retained or discarded to correctly depict the first purebred born in the United States. From the upright ears to the tip of the corkscrew tail, each element was analyzed and reviewed to preserve only those features that best represented this new breed. Since 1891, when the first standard was drafted and later accepted by the American Kennel Club (AKC), fanciers have selected only those specimens with proper breed type to perpetuate this one-of-a-kind canine who is known—and cherished—worldwide as the Boston Terrier.

PHYSICAL CHARACTERISTICS

The key to this breed is balance. When viewed from the side, the Boston is square in appearance, as the length of his body matches his height at the withers. His head, which also forms a square, rests atop a gracefully arched neck set neatly into sloping shoulders. His topline is level, while the rump forms a curve to the base of the tail. Straight forelegs with strong wrists, combined with well-muscled hindquarters, drive his powerful yet rhythmic gait. Some call the Boston a large dog in a small body, as he conveys a sense of activity, determination, and strength wrapped up in a perfectly proportioned package.

To read the full standard, which was revised in 2011, log on to the website of the Boston Terrier Club of America (BTCA) at www.bostonterrierclubofamerica.org.

SIZE

The Boston competes in the show ring in one of three weight divisions: under 15 pounds (7 kg), 15 pounds and under 20 pounds (7 and 9 kg), or 20 pounds and not more than 25 pounds (9 and 11.5 kg). Regardless of weight, he must display the compact, sturdy, and square appearance called for by the standard. (Females may be slightly more refined and delicate.) A well-built Boston should never be blocky, chunky, or spindly (fine boned). Note that neither the AKC nor the BTCA recognizes "teacup" Bostons. Full-grown dogs weighing less than 10 pounds (4.5 kg) may be predisposed to a variety of health problems, as well as more susceptible to accidents and injuries.

COAT AND COLORS

In his short, sleek, and smooth coat with markings that suggest he is outfitted for a black-tie affair, this little fellow dresses with the savoir faire worthy of his Beacon Hill brethren. The only acceptable colors for the breed, once called the "black satin gentleman," are brindle, seal, or black, with white markings.

Bostons must have white muzzle bands, white blazes between the eyes, and white forechests.

Brindle

Brindle is a pattern, rather than a color, in which layers of black hair cover a lighter shade underneath to form an irregular array of stripes throughout the coat. (Brindle and white is preferred over seal or black but only if the dog is equal in all other respects.)

Seal

Seal appears black but takes on a red cast when viewed in bright light or direct sunlight.

Black

Black is the least common shade, surprisingly, as most Bostons who look pure black actually have some degree of brindling in their coats.

Markings

Bostons must have white muzzle bands, white blazes between the eyes, and white forechests. Desired markings stipulate white muzzle bands, even white blazes between the eyes and over the head, white collars and forechests, and white on at least part of the forelegs and below the hocks (ankles) of the hind legs. Those who lack the required markings are called "undermarked"; too much white, "overmarked"; and white or dark in the wrong places, "mismarked." White-factored dogs are mostly white with irregular dark patches. Some Bostons develop pigment spots on the skin beneath their white markings and less frequently under the dark regions. These occur in some bloodlines more than others and are thought to be related to aging and sun exposure.

Non-Standard Colors

In your quest for the perfect Boston, you may have encountered breeders who advertise their red, blue, fawn, or cream puppies as sufficiently rare to command high prices from buyers who are unfamiliar with the standard. Some fail to perform even minimal health testing of their breeding stock, selecting on the basis of color alone. Of course, because the genes responsible for such colors are recessive and may be carried for generations without being expressed, any puppy might *accidentally* be born with a non-standard coat color or marking pattern. However, responsible breeders would neuter such a puppy and not attempt to perpetuate the unexpected result as a desirable trait.

HEAD

Known for his alert and kind expression, which shows a high degree of intelligence, the Boston's head sets him apart from all other breeds. In fact, his head, eyes, and ears so define the Boston that they make up a quarter of the points allotted by the standard. Starting with his square-shaped skull, which is flat on top—never domed—his cheeks lie neatly against his short, wide muzzle. His jaw is broad and square, with an even or slightly undershot bite. Neither his forehead nor his muzzle bears the wrinkles that characterize his Bulldog and French Bulldog cousins. From Barnard's Mike, born more than a century ago, he inherited his full, round eyes, which are wide-set and dark in color. His nose is black, with a well-defined line between the nostrils. An indentation, or "stop," is visible above the bridge of his nose. Finally, his ears, which may be cropped or naturally erect, are set as closely as possible to the corners of his skull to further enhance the symmetry of his head.

The Boston's small, upright ears are set as closely as possible to the corners of his skull to further enhance the symmetry of his head.

TAIL

A distinctive feature of the breed, the tail is naturally short—never docked—set low on the rump and tapering at the tip. It may be straight or screw-shaped—twisted in a spiral formation that resembles a corkscrew. The first Bostons wagged straight tails. However, Barnard's Tom, a grandson of Hooper's Judge, was born with the breed's first screw tail. "Tom in the nest looked to be the perfect dog—but horror of horrors, the dogs in those days had straight tails of much more than moderate length, but the puppy, Tom, possessed a screw tail," recounted dog author Vincent Perry. "[John P. Barnard] took the puppy to a vet surgeon with

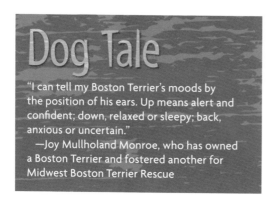

the request that the tail be put in splints in an effort to straighten it out. 'It cannot be done' was the verdict of the vet and so started the craze for the kink in the tails of our American dog."

LIVING WITH YOUR BOSTON

Not only do Boston Terriers differ from one another in their physical characteristics—from body build and size to color and markings—but also in their personalities, exercise requirements, and trainability. Each is a unique individual, and that's what owners love about their pets. Diversity among Bostons arises from both nature, the genetic makeup of the parents, as well as nurture, the early socialization and stimulation that puppies receive in their first critical months. To find the ideal Boston who fits your lifestyle, let the breeder know the overall plans you have for your dog. Are you seeking a couch companion, or do you prefer engaging in active sports? Are young children or other pets in the household? Would obedience training and competition interest you?

Be sure to visit the breeder in person so that you can observe whether the sire and dam exhibit the traits you hope to find in your puppy. Don't overlook an adolescent, adult, or even a senior, whose disposition is already established and known. Or—better yet—contact one of the rescue organizations whose volunteers are dedicated to fostering and placing Bostons who find themselves homeless through no fault of their own.

PERSONALITY

Loving and loyal, small and compact, Bostons are just the right size to sit on your lap, snuggle under the covers, or accompany you on your daily excursions. These happy-go-lucky fellows thrive on human companionship and always manage to find themselves in the midst of the action. With their lively facial expressions and playful body language, Bostons delight young and old alike with their clown-like antics. From comical games to cute tricks, they display an impish sense of humor. Simply laugh, and they will gleefully repeat whatever brought about such approval. Owners who channel this enthusiasm and willingness to please into obedience training and performance sports find that Bostons excel

Loving and loyal, small and compact, Bostons are just the right size to sit on your lap, snuggle under the covers, or accompany you on your daily excursions.

in agility, flyball, rally, and other forms of competition. In fact, their intelligence, coupled with their near-human sensitivity, leads many owners to proclaim that once you have shared your home with a Boston, no other breed will do.

COMPANIONABILITY

"A more devoted family dog never was born," said Jill Ritchey of Sunwoods Kennel, who readily admits that her husband married her so that he could be a "father" to Luke, her first Boston Terrier champion. Bred for more than a century for their outgoing and sociable temperaments, Bostons are people-oriented dogs who need a great deal of affection and attention. They fare poorly if left alone for hours on end, and in fact the cruelest form of punishment is to isolate them. Many owners—especially those with full-time jobs—have doubled their pleasure by adding a second Boston to keep the first one company.

With Children

Fun loving and spirited yet gentle and kindhearted, Bostons make wonderful playmates for children of all ages. Whether engaging in rough-and-tumble games or offering their furry shoulders to cry on, Bostons have the remarkable ability to sense their charges' moods and adjust their behavior accordingly. Of course, close supervision of children and pets is essential to maintain a harmonious relationship: No pulling of ears or poking of vulnerable eyes allowed! Parents must teach youngsters that dogs are not playthings but living creatures who require kindness, patience, and understanding to thrive.

With Dogs

Bostons like to interact with breeds large and small—especially at the dog park—but prefer their own kind whenever possible. Games of chase and tug-of-war entertain for hours, followed by restorative naps all around. A favorite activity is "bitey-face," in which they engage as often as possible. This mock-fighting pastime involves open-mouthed biting and face bumping, accompanied by an array of loud, vicious-sounding noises. Although it's understood to be playful by all participants, be sure to monitor and stop bitey-face with a firm "Enough!" if it becomes too rowdy. Keep in mind that this flat-faced, short-nosed breed emits all kinds of sounds—from growls and grumbles to snorts and snuffles—during vigorous toy attacks. While not big barkers, they nonetheless can be brash enough at times to concern those unfamiliar with the breed's vocalizations.

Many owners— especially those with full-time jobs—have doubled their pleasure by adding a second Boston to keep the first one company.

ENVIRONMENT

As long as they are with their families, Bostons are adaptable to any environment—from city apartments with nearby parks to country estates with acres to roam. Their clean habits and good manners suit the most formal decor, but even with minimal shedding, be prepared for a few black and white hairs to cling to furniture and carpets. Many owners protect upholstered surfaces with washable slipcovers and install scratch- and stain-resistant laminate or tile flooring. If staircases and stairwells pose a hazard, close them off with doggy gates. Crates, gates, and exercise pens are indispensable in keeping your Boston safe whenever you're unable to provide close supervision. Fortunately, Bostons are not choosy about their accommodations and make themselves at home in any surroundings.

EXERCISE

Each Boston differs in the amount and type of exercise he prefers, but most have moderate to high energy levels. Lively enough to be playful without being hyperactive, Bostons love to retrieve balls, enjoy 30- to 45-minute daily walks, and look forward to all-out runs in the safety of enclosed dog parks. Perhaps you have witnessed their distinctive racing style, nicknamed the "BT 500" for its resemblance to the full-speed laps taken by race cars on oval tracks. With

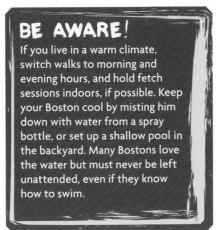

BE AWARE!

If you live in a warm climate, switch walks to morning and evening hours, and hold fetch sessions indoors, if possible. Keep your Boston cool by misting him down with water from a spray bottle, or set up a shallow pool in the backyard. Many Bostons love the water but must never be left unattended, even if they know how to swim.

their ears slicked back, eyes bugged out, and hindquarters tucked under, Bostons run full-tilt in loops throughout the house or yard. With more than one involved, dogs mimic the rollicking bump-and-run manner of NASCAR. "My dog is so happy during and after a BT 500," said Erika Griffiths, of her dog Trevor. "I can tell by his huge grin with his tongue hanging out."

TRAINABILITY

From the fast pace of agility to the precise execution of formal obedience, Bostons are smart and creative problem solvers. They love to learn, retain their training, and understand a large vocabulary. The key is consistency and repetition but without the constant drilling necessary with other breeds. Turn lessons into a game and the task becomes a challenge to be mastered. Discover what motivates your dog—usually food but perhaps a special toy—and reward

each achievement rather than punishing his mistakes. More sensitive to their owners' tone of voice than some breeds, Bostons wilt under harsh correction and their dismay is obvious by their flattened ears and hurt demeanor. Remember that your Boston Terrier is trying his best to do whatever is asked of him. With clear rules and proper guidance he will ultimately succeed.

Most Bostons have moderate to high energy levels.

CHARACTERISTICS OF YOUR BOSTON TERRIER

SUPPLIES FOR YOUR
BOSTON TERRIER

The Boston's favorite place to sleep is in the bed he shares with his owner!

Now that you have decided the Boston Terrier is the right breed for you and you've located a reputable kennel with available puppies, it's time to go shopping for the adorable boy or girl who will soon be joining your household. If you're a first-time dog owner, the array of merchandise displayed on the shelves of your local pet supply store may be overwhelming. Bowls of every size, collars of every hue, and beds of every style make up a fraction of the $11 billion spent each year on pet products in the United States. Fortunately, puppies need only a few basics as they settle into their new homes. There will be plenty of time later to purchase luxury items if you so desire. Be sure to check for the best prices, whether you shop at brick-and-mortar establishments, online, or by mail order. Don't overlook small businesses—a number of dog-owning vendors make and sell specialty products with Bostons in mind.

BED

The Boston's favorite place to sleep is in the bed he shares with his owner. Nonetheless, he also needs his own dog bed for relaxation and the occasional siesta. Because puppies find de-stuffing their beds an amusing pastime, you may want to provide an indestructible blanket until your youngster outgrows the chewing stage. When you select his first big-dog bed, consider his sleeping style— does he curl into a ball or stretch out for slumber? Bostons who curl up prefer fluffy donut or bucket beds, whereas those who sprawl enjoy pillow or beanbag styles. Add a fleece blanket for extra warmth. A particular favorite is a custom-made plush-lined, open-ended sleeping bag that serves as both a bed and blanket. Look for a removable machine-washable cover, and buy an extra cover to use on laundry day. Other bed styles include orthopedic mattresses for dogs with joint problems, as well as heated or cooling beds—even canine waterbeds. To find the correct size, measure your Boston when he's stretched out and add about 1 foot (.5 m) in length. If you have multiple dogs, expect everyone to cuddle together on an extra-large cushion. Place the bed in a sunny spot, and soon you'll hear the familiar sound of blissful snoring.

CLOTHING

When the weather gets chilly, the American Gentleman needs more than his built-in tuxedo to keep him warm. A coat or sweater is essential—not merely a fashion statement—for this shorthaired breed that can't tolerate the cold. Look for jackets with water-resistant outer fabric and fleece or quilted linings. Coats may be easier to put on and take off than over-the-head sweaters, but some Bostons wear both in truly frigid climates. To ensure a proper fit, have your Boston try on clothing in the store or look for sizes based on chest and back

A coat or sweater is essential—not merely a fashion statement—for this shorthaired breed that can't tolerate the cold.

"I noticed that my Boston's flat nylon collar was causing irritation and hair loss under his neck. When I switched to a rolled leather collar—expensive but it lasts a lifetime—the problem cleared up in a few weeks."
—Gabe Ugolini, who shares his home with two Boston Terriers

measurements rather than weight alone. Other choices include rain slickers to stay dry in downpours and cooling vests to guard against overheating during the "dog days" of summer. Elderly pets appreciate soft tee shirts or cozy pajamas on winter evenings. Remember that even a formally clad fellow requires a practical outfit in his wardrobe.

COLLAR

Dogs have worn collars—for identification and training purposes—since the early Egyptians first adorned their hounds more than 5,000 years ago. In fact, as highly prized collectibles, antique dog collars have their own Dog Collar Museum inside England's Leeds Castle. Your Boston, however, requires only a standard collar for his daily walks.

If you're worried about your Boston slipping his collar or prefer greater control during walks, consider using a harness.

Several styles are available:

- *Buckle collars* come in cotton, leather, and nylon and fasten with buckle closures. They have a ring to hold tags and often include a separate ring for the leash clip. Fabric collars may be embroidered with your pet's name and telephone number, in case he loses his ID tag. Others offer reflective stripes for added visibility after dark. Look for a narrow, rolled-leather collar if flat styles irritate your Boston's neck.
- *Quick-release collars* are adjustable fabric collars with plastic or metal spring clasps that make them easy to put on and remove in a hurry.
- *Breakaway collars* feature special connectors that release under pressure to prevent choking if they snag on objects. To keep the collar from opening during walks, attach the leash to both rings so that it straddles the connector.
- *Martingale collars* are composed of two loops—one that goes around your dog's neck and the other that clips to his leash—to form a snug fit that prevents escape during walks.

To find the correct size, measure your Boston's neck and add 2 inches (5 cm). Two fingers should easily slip between his collar and neck. Some owners put on collars only when their pets are outside. If you plan to use one all the time, try a breakaway collar that releases in an emergency.

HARNESS

If you're worried about your Boston slipping his collar or prefer greater control during walks, consider using a harness. Dogs who pull on their leashes may exert enough pressure on their collars to hurt their throats, but harnesses direct those forces to the chest and shoulder areas instead. Keep in mind that only proper training will solve a pulling problem. In fact, without training, a harness may make it worse by allowing a dog to pull harder. Harnesses, like collars, come in an array of materials and styles. Look for an adjustable harness—Puppia and Harness Heaven earn the Boston seal of approval—that is both durable and comfortable to wear.

CRATE

A wire crate is convenient to fold down for travel, whereas an airline-style carrier is easy to keep clean and sanitized. Be sure that the crate is the correct size. Some owners purchase crates that are too large so that their dogs will have plenty of room. However, this defeats the crates' purpose for housetraining because puppies have enough space to relieve themselves and still keep their beds clean. Look for a small crate (24"L × 18"W × 21"H [61 cm L × 45.5 cm W × 53.5 cm H]) for Bostons up to 25 pounds (11.5 kg) or a medium crate (30"L × 21"W × 24"H [76 cm L × 53.5 cm W × 61 cm H]) for those up to 40 pounds (18 kg). Some crates include dividers so that you can adjust the size of your dog's living quarters as he grows.

EX-PEN

An exercise pen (ex-pen) is an effective way to keep your puppy corralled when you're too busy to monitor his activities. Made of separate wire panels that fold flat for storage, ex-pens can be set up to enclose a space of any size or stretched out to block off no-trespassing zones in an open floor plan. (Place a piece of old carpeting under the pen to protect flooring.) Popular at dog shows, ex-pens can also be used to confine pets when outdoors. Add a top for safety if your Boston likes to climb or jump out. Place his bed and toys, along with food and water, inside, and your Boston Terrier will be content to rest or play by himself.

FOOD AND WATER BOWLS

Dog feeders range from stainless steel, ceramic, and plastic bowls to elevated dishes and automatic dispensers. You'll need two bowls: one for food and the other for water. Bostons are prone to overheating when playing outdoors, so buy an extra bowl for the backyard and keep it filled with water or ice cubes. A portable water bottle for trips to the dog park will also come in handy.

Choose a set of medium-sized bowls that are wide and shallow so that your Boston can pick up kibble and drink more easily. If he chows down so rapidly that he develops flatulence, look for an anti-gulping bowl with bumps in the center to slow down his eating. Most owners use stainless steel bowls, which are easy to clean, dishwasher safe, and unbreakable. Ceramic dishes are heavy and less likely to spill but may chip or crack over time. Plastic bowls are practical and inexpensive but tend to retain

Most owners use stainless steel bowls, which are easy to clean, dishwasher safe, and unbreakable.

food oils and harbor bacteria that cause facial acne in some Bostons.

Automatic food dispensers are convenient if you're unable to be home at dinnertime, but free-feeding often results in obesity in dogs who can't adequately regulate their consumption. Automatic waterers, however, work well—especially in multiple-dog households.

Always keep bowls spotlessly clean, especially if you feed a raw foods–based diet.

GATE

You'll want to confine your Boston to rooms with washable floors until he is fully housetrained. A gate not only blocks doorways to off-limits areas but also guards against falls down open stairwells. Made of plastic, metal, and wood, dog gates range from 2 to 4 feet (.5 to 1 m) in height. Walk-through styles are more convenient than are those you must step over. Select a tall gate for a vigorous jumper and steel slats if you have an aggressive chewer. Also, make certain that the bars are spaced together closely enough so that your puppy can't get his head stuck. Gates may be pressure mounted, which makes them easy to move from room to room; hardware mounted, for a permanent sturdy barrier; or freestanding, for blocking large open doorways. All puppies need to learn boundaries. A dog gate is an easy way to ensure your Boston's safety while allowing more freedom than confining him to a crate or ex-pen.

Your Boston should wear ID tags, as well as have a more permanent form of identification, such as a microchip.

IDENTIFICATION

Few things strike greater fear in the heart of a dog owner than discovering an open gate and realizing a pet is missing. Bostons are notorious escape artists, readily able to scale over or burrow under backyard fences, so it's important to properly identify your puppy as soon as you bring him home. ID tags have come a long way since the metal disks of yesteryear. Today, dogs can sport programmable digital tags and bone-shaped flash drives that store names, telephone numbers, and other vital information. GPS devices can be attached to collars as well, which enable owners to track their dogs' whereabouts online.

Because collars can break and tags become lost, be sure to ask your veterinarian about getting a microchip, which is inserted using a syringe under the skin between the shoulder blades. Microchips store unique codes that identify dogs and their owners. Most clinics and shelters have handheld scanners available to check lost and stray animals for the presence of chips. If one is detected, a 24-hour hotline tracks down the owner. Remember that your Boston can't give his address if he gets lost. A collar with an ID tag, backed up by a microchip, is vital in helping him find his way back home.

LEASH

Often made of the same materials as their coordinating collars and harnesses, leashes come in a variety of cotton, leather, and nylon styles. Fabric leashes, which are lightweight but strong, are ideal for puppy training. Leather is a bit heavier but softens over time to become a durable leash that will last a lifetime. Sizes range from 1/2 to 1 inch (1.5 to 2.5 cm) in width and 4 to 6 feet (1 to 2 m) in length. (Most classes require a 6-foot [2-m] cotton or nylon leash for training purposes.) To give your Boston extra freedom, try a retractable leash that extends up to 26 feet (8 m). A button on the handle lets you stop at any point. This type of leash provides added security when teaching the *come* and *stay* commands but offers little control in an emergency. Also, the cables may become tangled if a group of owners are walking their dogs together. Other styles are designed for hands-free use when jogging or riding a bicycle. Review your community's leash laws, and keep your Boston safe and secure at all times.

Bostons are easy to please when it comes to toys and games that they enjoy.

REGISTRATION

When you purchase your puppy, be sure that you receive the American Kennel Club (AKC) Dog Registration Application (blue slip). If you plan to compete in dog shows, you'll need to obtain full registration from the breeder. This also allows future offspring to qualify for registration if you decide to breed your Boston at a later date. However, most breeders sell their pet-quality puppies with limited registration privileges, which permit Bostons to enter all companion and performance events— except conformation. Because limited

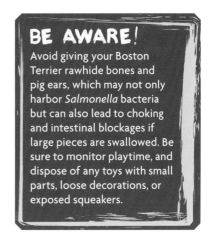

BE AWARE!

Avoid giving your Boston Terrier rawhide bones and pig ears, which may not only harbor *Salmonella* bacteria but can also lead to choking and intestinal blockages if large pieces are swallowed. Be sure to monitor playtime, and dispose of any toys with small parts, loose decorations, or exposed squeakers.

registration prevents puppies from parents with conformation faults from being registered, it's one measure that breeders take to protect their dogs from falling into the hands of individuals who may not have the Boston's welfare as a top priority. The AKC also grants a Purebred Alternative Listing/Indefinite Listing Privilege (PAL/ILP) number to unregistered dogs, such as rescue animals, so that they may participate in the same events as those with limited registration.

TOYS

Bostons are easy to please when it comes to their toy boxes. They love chasing balls, de-stuffing plush toys, and playing tug-of-war with their pals. Because they are powerful chewers with strong jaws, it's essential to provide safe, durable toys—and to monitor their play at all times.

Favorites include items that make noise, treat-dispensing toys, and sturdy chews. They enjoy fetching racquet or squash balls, but tennis balls are easily shredded. For hours of chewing delight, try bully sticks or commercially prepared deer antlers. (Give chew toys only when you can supervise your dog.) If you want to offer a special treat, try one of the chewies made of compressed vegetable ingredients. Their small, easy-to-digest particles allow pets to consume them safely.

For more toy ideas for your Boston, visit the Boston Terrier Challenge Dog Toy Test (www.boston-terrier-challenge.com), which rates toys on their fun factor and durability as judged by Boston volunteers. The website www.healthystuff.org evaluates pet products for the presence of toxic chemicals.

FEEDING YOUR BOSTON TERRIER

Food provides the basic building blocks that help the Boston Terrier reach his full potential. It forms strong bones and teeth, keeps his skin and coat in peak condition, builds muscle, and—most importantly—nourishes every cell in his body to help him live a long and active life. Whether you choose commercial kibble or a home-cooked meal, his diet must offer complete and balanced nutrition for his stage of development—puppy, adult, or senior. Your Boston's well-being is in your hands.

Your dog draws upon his carb reserves when he needs a quick burst of energy.

BASIC NUTRIENTS

Your Boston needs six kinds of nutrients for optimal health: carbohydrates, fat, minerals, protein, vitamins, and water. The term "nutrient" refers to any factor that aids in the body's metabolic processes. The amount and balance of these nutrients will differ, however, based on your pet's age and activity level, environment, and general health.

CARBOHYDRATES

Grains, along with fruits and vegetables, fuel your Boston's daily activities. Carbohydrates come in two forms, simple and complex, based on the size of their molecules. Simple carbs are sugars—sucrose, fructose, and lactose—that are transformed by the liver into glycogen and stored for later use. Your dog draws upon these reserves when he needs a quick burst of energy. Glucose also plays a critical role in nourishing the brain because it's one of the few substances that can cross the blood–brain barrier. Complex carbs, including whole grains, vegetables, legumes, and potatoes, are rich in fiber and travel more slowly through the digestive tract than do simple sugars. Some forms are useful when dogs have diarrhea or constipation. Others help to lower the level of cholesterol in the blood. Because fiber also decreases the absorption of nutrients, puppies and active adults should avoid diets high in roughage. Bostons are sensitive to grains, and some fare better on grain-free diets.

FAT

Dietary fat offers a concentrated source of energy when your puppy is rapidly growing, and it helps active dogs maintain their body mass. Saturated fats are solid at room temperature and come from animal sources, whereas unsaturated fats are derived from plants and remain liquid at room temperature. Fat not only makes food taste better but also enables the absorption of fat-soluble vitamins. Fat keeps the skin and coat healthy, contributes to a properly functioning nervous system, and is a building block for a variety of hormones.

Most dogs need diets that contain between 8 and 20 percent fat. Too little may cause weight loss, fatigue, and poor wound healing. Too much, however, leads to obesity, steatorrhea (undigested fat passed in the stool), and pancreatitis (inflammation of the pancreas).

MINERALS

Making up less than 1 percent of your Boston's weight, minerals perform several important functions. Macrominerals, including calcium, magnesium, potassium, sodium, and chloride, are required in larger amounts than are trace minerals, such as iron, zinc, and selenium. Calcium, for example, builds strong bones and teeth. Other macrominerals regulate the blood's acid–base balance, maintain the proper amount of water in cells, and influence the action of nerves and muscles. Trace elements help to form hemoglobin, which transports oxygen throughout the body, and these minerals also assist the immune system in healing wounds and fending off infections.

Dogs need a specific balance of minerals, which most pet foods supply. Adding minerals, especially calcium and phosphorus, may upset this balance, leading to lameness, fractures, and abnormal bone development.

Fat in the diet helps keep the skin and coat healthy.

PROTEIN

Found in foods like beef, poultry, fish, eggs, and grains, protein is vital for growth and development. Keratin, one type of protein, makes up the basic structure of skin, hair, and nails. Collagen, another form, constitutes connective tissue, such as tendons, ligaments, and muscles. As food is digested, protein is broken down into smaller substances called amino acids. Carried by the bloodstream, amino acids help to build and repair tissue, as well as aid in the production of antibodies, hemoglobin, and certain hormones. Dogs need 22 amino acids and can produce a dozen within their own bodies. The other ten are known as essential amino acids because they must be supplied by the diet. Most pet foods use a variety of ingredients to ensure that they provide a complete source of protein.

Puppies, who grow rapidly during their first year, need diets that contain between 25 and 30 percent protein. Adults require about 22 percent. Too little protein may lead to skeletal disorders, weight loss, skin and coat problems, and lowered resistance to disease, whereas too much could be harmful to those with impaired kidney or liver function.

VITAMINS

First identified at the dawn of the 20th century, vitamins are organic compounds that help to regulate many bodily processes. Vitamins are classified into two groups—fat soluble and water soluble—based on how they are absorbed, stored, and excreted. The four fat-soluble vitamins are A, D, E, and K. As their name suggests, these are stored in the body's fat reserves and liver—from a few days to several months—until needed. Vitamins A, D, E, and K play important roles, respectively, in eyesight, building strong bones and teeth, protecting tissues, and helping blood to properly clot. Because they are not readily excreted, fat-soluble vitamins can build up to

Puppies, who grow rapidly during their first year, need diets that contain between 25 and 30 percent protein.

Be sure that your dog has easy access to his water bowl, and refill it at least once a day.

potentially harmful levels if given in large amounts. Water-soluble vitamins—B complex and C—make hormones, carry oxygen, and fight infection. They become depleted more quickly and must be regularly replaced.

WATER

Fresh, clean drinking water is the most important nutrient for your Boston. Water is necessary for digestion and elimination of body wastes, lubricating the joints, maintaining healthy cells, and regulating body temperature. Although dogs can survive for days without food, a loss of only 10 to 15 percent of body water can cause illness and even death.

Dogs obtain water from drinking and the water content of their food, as well as from various metabolic processes. Their thirst response increases or decreases based on activity level, metabolism, and even weather conditions.

Be sure that your dog has easy access to his water bowl, and refill it at least once a day. Consider using a filter if the quality of your local water supply is less than ideal. Take a water bottle along on walks or trips to the dog park because Bostons are susceptible to overheating and may become dehydrated in warm weather. Dogs usually self-regulate their fluid intake based on the outflow from urination, panting, vomiting, or diarrhea. However, if you notice that your Boston is drinking more or less than usual, consult his veterinarian.

COMMERCIAL FOOD

Since the first mass-produced doggy biscuit rolled off the conveyor belt in the late 19th century, breeders and owners, along with veterinarians, have worked to define canine nutritional requirements and formulate appropriate foods to meet those needs. The Association of American Feed Control Officials (AAFCO) sets the standards by which pet foods may be labeled "complete and balanced." Companies meet this requirement either by submitting a nutrient analysis or by conducting feeding trials. The AAFCO certifies formulas for both puppies and adults. Today, the pet food industry has grown to become a multibillion-dollar-a-year business. With more than 300 manufacturers annually producing 7 million tons of pet food, how can you choose the best diet from the vast array of dry, canned, and semi-moist varieties?

DRY FOOD (KIBBLE)

Introduced in the 1860s as an offshoot of the cereal industry, dry food—or kibble—is the most popular method of feeding today. Meat meal, grains, and vegetables are the primary ingredients, with extra fat, vitamins, and minerals added after baking. Dry food is affordable, readily available, and easy to prepare and store. Its low water content means that you pay only for the food itself, rather than for fancy packaging.

Dry food is affordable, readily available, and easy to prepare and store.

Kibble comes in numerous formulations—from salmon-and-potato to bison-and-rice—along with small or large nuggets and even diets for specific breeds. (Bostons don't yet have their own food.) Quality ranges from human-grade ingredients to economy brands that contain fillers, sugars, and artificial colors. Premium foods may cost more per unit of weight but are nutrient-dense, so your dog requires less food overall. Use the portion recommendations only as a starting point. Your Boston may need more or less food than the label suggests.

The best choice in kibble is one that your dog likes and thrives on, not necessarily the costliest. A well-nourished Boston sports a glossy coat and healthy skin, clear bright eyes, and small, solid stools. On the right diet, he has almost no flatulence.

When purchasing dry food, always check the expiration date and make certain that the bag is undamaged. Brands that use a natural preservative, such as vitamin E, have shorter shelf lives than do those with BHA, BHT, or ethoxyquin. Always store kibble in a sealed container in a cool, dry place.

CANNED FOOD

Canned food contains more water than dry or semi-moist and may be more expensive to feed on a daily basis. Two forms—all meat and ration—are available. Meat meals contain up to 95 percent meat and meat by-products, along with vitamins and minerals. They work well for active dogs who need high-energy foods and for those who can't tolerate grains. Small amounts may also be added to dry food to improve its flavor. Canned rations, on the other hand, offer a balance of meat, carbohydrates, dietary fat, vitamins, and minerals. Recipes are available for puppies, adults, and seniors. A number of premium brands look and taste like human-grade stew, with an appealing mixture of meat and vegetables.

Be sure to keep opened cans in the refrigerator, and don't leave uneaten food in your dog's bowl.

SEMI-MOIST FOOD

Shaped like hamburger patties or meat chunks, semi-moist foods offer adequate nutrition in easy-to-use pouches. These single-serving meals need no refrigeration, travel well, and have a fairly long shelf life. However, most contain sugar, artificial flavoring and coloring, preservatives, and humectants to prevent drying out. Bostons may be particularly sensitive to these additives and develop diarrhea. Be sure that the cellophane wrapping is intact before feeding because contact with air can cause the food to deteriorate or become rancid.

THERAPEUTIC FOOD

The food your Boston eats plays a critical role in the management and treatment of certain diseases. For example, dogs with acute kidney disease require diets with lower levels of high-quality protein, whereas those with heart failure need reduced-sodium foods. Dogs with dry and itchy skin, allergies, joint disorders, and age-related problems also benefit from specially balanced formulas. To make therapeutic feeding simpler and more convenient, researchers have teamed up with pet food manufacturers to create an assortment of dry and canned products, available by prescription from veterinarians. With the right food, you can take a significant step in improving your Boston's health and longevity.

NON-COMMERCIAL FOOD

Because of concerns over the quality and safety of pet food ingredients—particularly since the 2007 recall of more than 150 brands—a growing number of owners have elected to prepare their Boston's dinner from scratch. Veterinarians also recommend homemade diets for pets with complex illnesses for which no commercial diet is satisfactory, or for seriously ill dogs who won't eat their usual kibble. Home cooking and raw feeding may require more effort than providing commercial products, but they enable owners to keep track of exactly what is going into their pets' diets.

HOME-COOKED DIET

Everyone enjoys a home-cooked meal—meat and potatoes, with a side of vegetables. Our dogs, too, prefer a tasty meal to their standard fare. To ensure that your Boston receives optimal nutrition, it's important to select from a variety of fresh ingredients. Protein sources include beef, poultry, fish, and eggs. Vegetables, such as broccoli, squash, peas, carrots, green beans, and sweet potato, provide carbohydrates for energy. Grains, if tolerated, add fiber to improve digestion. Home-cooked diets need to be supplemented with vitamins and minerals. If you're willing to make the commitment in time, energy, and added expense to cook for your Boston, be sure to obtain a scientifically based guidebook and follow the recipes exactly. Wendy Orgren, a breeder with more than 35 years' experience raising and showing Boston Terriers, offers nutritionally balanced recipes for a fee on her website (www.boston-terriers.com/dogsalive.htm). These have been tested extensively on her show dogs, as well as on other breeds. Your veterinarian may also recommend a diet that provides complete and balanced nutrition.

RAW DIET

Advocates of raw feeding believe that the high temperatures used in commercial processing destroy vital nutrients, making a raw diet a better alternative

Many raw diet advocates believe that their dogs have fewer tearstains and shinier coats than do dogs fed other diets.

for health and well-being. One popular plan goes by the acronym "BARF," which stands for "Bones and Raw Food" or "Biologically Appropriate Raw Food." By feeding an evolutionary diet like that consumed by our canines' wild ancestors—based on raw muscle meat, organs, meaty bones, vegetables, and fruit—supporters suggest that pets can enjoy a variety of benefits. "Switching to a raw diet was the best thing we have done," said Natacha Dagenais Rodrigue and Lynn Dagenais, of their crew of four Bostons. "No more tearstains, nice shiny coats, small, solid stools, and no more flatulence. It's absolutely amazing the results in feeding a species-appropriate raw diet."

Three feeding methods are available: home-prepared meals, grain products to which uncooked meat is added, and prepackaged frozen or freeze-dried foods that need no further supplementation. Raw feeding can be more costly than other plans, especially in multiple-dog households. (To save money, buy ingredients in bulk and create your own portions.) It's also harder to maintain a raw diet if you and your dog frequently travel.

Although many Bostons do quite well on this diet, the American Veterinary

Medical Association (AVMA) warns about the possible presence of bacteria, such as *Salmonella* and *E. coli*, as well as parasites in uncooked meat. Be sure to thoroughly clean all surfaces that come into contact with raw meat, especially your dog's food and water bowls. Experts recommend soaking bowls in a 10-percent chlorine solution for several minutes after a basic cleaning with dish soap. Dogs—and people—with compromised immune systems are more vulnerable to illnesses caused by bacterial contamination.

In fact, in 2010, the Delta Society prohibited dogs who consume uncooked animal-based proteins or raw bones from participating in its Pet Partners therapy program. The group determined that the population it serves might be at greater risk by interacting with dogs from households that feed a raw diet. Always check with your veterinarian before making major changes to your Boston's diet.

SUPPLEMENTS

With the selection of supplements displayed on pet store shelves, it's natural to wonder whether your dog would benefit from an extra boost to his nutrition. This decision must be based on your individual Boston: the kind of diet he eats, his age and activity level, and his current health status.

ESSENTIAL FATTY ACIDS

Known as vitamin F, essential fatty acids (EFAs) impact the immune system and act as powerful anti-inflammatory agents. Dogs need linolenic acid (omega-3), along with linoleic and arachidonic (omega-6) acids. The ratio of omega-3 to omega-6 is important because the former inhibits inflammation, whereas the latter promotes it. The ideal ratio ranges from 1:2 to 1:10. Because pet food tends to be high in omega-6s, adding omega-3s brings these nutrients into balance. Wild salmon oil (not cod liver oil, which contains high levels of vitamins A and D) and flaxseed oil are excellent sources of omega-3. EFAs benefit dogs with skin and coat problems, allergies, joint disorders, and heart and kidney disease. Discuss supplementation with your veterinarian. Alpha-linolenic acid can thin the blood, and gamma-linolenic acid (found in borage oil) may cause seizures in susceptible dogs.

VITAMINS AND MINERALS

Most commercial foods provide the correct amount and balance of vitamins and minerals. However, if your dog consumes a home-cooked or raw diet, he may need a daily vitamin–mineral tablet. Antioxidants, substances that slow down cellular damage caused by free radicals, are particularly beneficial for seniors. Canine studies have shown that dogs who consume diets rich in vitamins C and E, beta-carotene, and selenium have fewer skin and coat problems, better immune function, and improvements in their ability to learn and remember. Check with your veterinarian for the correct dosage, and look for products with the National Animal Supplement Council (NASC) Seal of Quality. NASC members have submitted to audits of their facilities to ensure that its standards are being met.

Probiotics, available in foods such as yogurt, guard against infections and allergies, support the immune system, and may even reduce the risk of developing cancer.

PROBIOTICS

Old-time breeders who practiced adding a dollop of yogurt—which contains live cultures of "friendly" bacteria—to their dogs' diets may have been onto something. Probiotics, as these living beneficial microbes are called, reside in the gastrointestinal tract, where they compete against other, more harmful, organisms. Changes in diet and stress, as well as the use of antibiotics, may alter this balance. When harmful bacteria take over, dogs often develop diarrhea, constipation, vomiting, or food allergies. Probiotics not only decrease these problems but also confer a number of health benefits. They guard against infections and allergies, support the immune system, and may even reduce the risk of developing cancer. Probiotics also produce vitamins, such as biotin and folic acid, and complete the digestion of certain nutrients.

If your Boston's balance of healthy versus harmful bacteria has been compromised, consider adding probiotics to his diet in the form of tablets or powder sprinkled on his food. Choose a broad-spectrum agent that contains more than one strain. (No single form helps every problem.) It may take 10 to 14 days for probiotics to colonize the GI tract. Keep in mind that probiotics are living microbes, which may be killed by excessive heat or moisture, so store them in the refrigerator.

FOODS TO AVOID

Food	Active Component	Reactions
chocolate (from most to least toxic: cacao beans, cocoa powder, baking chocolate, dark and semisweet chocolate, milk and white chocolate)	theobromine, caffeine	vomiting, diarrhea, restlessness, panting, excessive thirst and urination, seizures, fast or irregular heartbeat, coma, death
grapes and raisins	unknown	acute kidney failure, death
macadamia nuts	unknown	muscle tremor, weakness, paralysis, pain, swelling, and stiffness in limbs
onions and garlic	thiosulphate	vomiting, diarrhea, breathing problems, hemolytic anemia
tomatoes (leaves and stems, green tomatoes)	tomatine, atropine	vomiting, diarrhea, breathing problems, muscle tremor, weakness, paralysis, irregular heartbeat, coma, death
Other foods to avoid include artificial sweeteners, coffee and tea, alcohol, fruit seeds and pits, raw fish, raw liver, raw egg whites, nutmeg, yeast dough, potatoes (green sprouts and green skin), and wild mushrooms.		

WHEN AND HOW TO FEED

Is dinnertime the favorite part of your Boston's day? Like people, dogs look forward to their meals, and they deserve to eat, undisturbed, in a quiet out-of-the-way place. Avoid petting or other interruptions when your Boston is eating. (However, all dogs should permit gentle handling without protest!) If you have multiple dogs who share (or steal) each other's food, try feeding each in his own crate.

When your new puppy comes home, the breeder should supply a feeding schedule and small bag of the food he has been eating. Puppies less than three months old usually need four meals per day at regular intervals. Maintaining a consistent schedule not only prevents your little one from becoming hungry but also makes housetraining easier. Puppies between 3 and 6 months of age should eat three times per day; between 6 and 12 months of age, two times.

If you decide to change pet foods, be sure to introduce the new diet over the course of several days. Rapid changes may lead to vomiting, constipation, or diarrhea.

Bostons sometimes have a tendency to vomit a yellow liquid when their stomachs are empty. This is because bile and acid build up and irritate the lining of the stomach. Feeding twice a day—morning and evening—usually solves this problem.

It's important to adhere to a regular feeding schedule. Free-feeding, in which a bowl of food is always available, doesn't work well with Bostons, who have difficulty regulating their intake. Some are prone to overeating, which leads to obesity and other health problems. And with more than one dog in the household, it's hard to know who is consuming more or less than he should. Free-feeding is safe only if you feed kibble because canned, raw, and home-cooked foods will spoil if left out for hours.

Usually, the cause of obesity in dogs is too much food and not enough exercise.

OBESITY

Following in the footsteps of their human companions, pets are facing an obesity crisis of their own. An estimated 25 to 40 percent of dogs in the United States—up to 15 million—are classified as obese. Obesity is the number-one nutritional disorder and fourth leading cause of death.

To tell if your Boston is fit, rub your hands over his ribs. Can you feel but not see them? From above, does his waist dip in? Is his belly nicely tucked up? Dogs are considered overweight at 5 to 19 percent over their ideal weight and obese at 20 percent. For a Boston who should weigh 15 pounds (7 kg), that's an excess of a mere 3 pounds (1.5 kg)!

If you suspect that your Boston needs to lose a few pounds (kg), have your veterinarian perform a thorough checkup. Certain medications and illnesses, such as Cushing's disease or low thyroid, may lead to weight gain. Usually, the cause is too much food and too little exercise. Your dog's veterinarian can suggest a reduced-calorie diet and exercise schedule. Helping your best friend become fit takes commitment and effort. You'll need to measure his food—he'll need about a quarter less daily to lose weight—and restrict snacks and treats. Baby carrots and green beans make appetizing low-cal snacks, and a nugget of kibble can be used as a reward for good behavior instead of a higher-calorie treat.

CHAPTER 5

GROOMING YOUR
BOSTON TERRIER

A dapper gentleman in his wash-and-wear tuxedo, the Boston Terrier has an easy-care coat that makes him a popular choice as both a family pet and show dog. Unlike many breeds whose flowing manes require daily attention and professional styling, this shorthaired dog thrives on a minimum of grooming. Simple brushing, bathing, and nail trimming form the basic routine. Add to that ear and eye care, along with regular tooth brushing, and you'll have a Boston who not only looks but also feels his best.

GROOMING AS A HEALTH CHECK

Our busy schedules often leave little time for grooming the family pet. However, investing just a few minutes each day can pay enormous dividends in your Boston's overall health. The time that you spend on grooming enables you to notice any physical changes and obtain treatment before they become more serious. Start each session by running your hands over your Boston's body. Are there any scrapes or scratches, lumps or bumps, evidence of fleas or ticks? Do his ears and eyes look healthy, his teeth pearly white? Do his toenails need trimming? A number of illnesses first show up in the eyes, skin, and coat, so it's important to detect problems early and bring them to the attention of your veterinarian.

The time that you spend on grooming enables you to notice any physical changes and obtain treatment early.

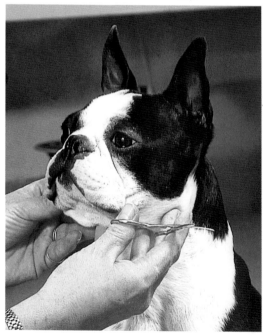

GROOMING SUPPLIES

To keep your Boston well groomed, you'll need the following supplies:
- baby wipes, unscented
- brush, soft bristle or rubber curry
- cotton balls
- dog shampoo
- dog toothbrush and toothpaste
- ear-cleaning solution or pads
- eye-cleaning solution or pads
- nail clippers or rotary grinder
- nail file or emery board
- paw wax (to protect footpads)
- spray nozzle attachment for the faucet
- styptic (blood-clotting) powder
- towels
- washcloth

COAT AND SKIN CARE

Bostons are patient little fellows when it comes to being groomed. They tolerate bath time and thrive on gentle brushing. In fact, grooming is a natural canine behavior. If you have multiple dogs, you'll often see one licking and cleaning the other. The secret to a cooperative Boston is to make grooming fun for both of you. Keep sessions brief, and always maintain a positive attitude. Give plenty of praise and perhaps a treat for good behavior. Before long, your Boston will be fetching his brush instead of his ball!

BRUSHING

Your Boston's coat is naturally tidy, but don't overlook the value of weekly brushing. Whether you prefer a soft-bristled brush or rubber curry, brushing stimulates blood circulation to bring vital nutrients to the hair follicles. It also distributes natural oils along each hair shaft to make the coat both shiny and water-resistant. A thorough brushing before bathing loosens dandruff flakes for easy removal and catches any shed hairs before they land on your clothes or furniture.

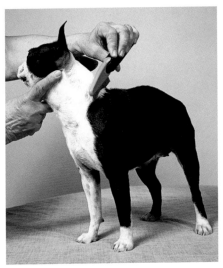

Keep grooming sessions brief, and always maintain a positive attitude with your Boston.

How to Brush Your Boston

To introduce your puppy to brushing, gently rub his body with a washcloth or the cloth side of a grooming mitt. Use an upbeat tone of voice and offer praise for his efforts.

1. Before you begin, put a rubber mat down on your grooming table (or other convenient surface) to prevent slipping. Place your Boston on the grooming table.
2. Start with his neck and back, brushing in the direction of hair growth.
3. Brush his front and back legs, down to his toes.
4. Next, brush his chest and belly.
5. Finish by carefully wiping his head, muzzle, and ears with a washcloth or grooming mitt.

   Never leave your Boston unattended on a grooming table.

SHEDDING

Dogs maintain their coats through a continual process of renewal. As old hair shafts die, they are shed to allow a new healthy coat to emerge. Light exposure affects the shedding cycle, along with stress, certain illnesses, hormonal changes, dietary deficiencies, and parasites. Because they are single-coated and lack a fluffy undercoat, Bostons shed less than many other breeds do. They go through a shedding cycle twice a year, in spring and fall, which lasts about a month. Otherwise, hair loss is minimal. Because the skin and coat reflect your Boston's overall health, contact your veterinarian if you

Brush your Boston daily with a soft-bristled brush or rubber curry.

notice more shedding than usual, dandruff, or bald patches.

How to Control Shedding

Minimizing shedding not only prevents a flurry of black and white fur from covering clothing and carpets but also readies the coat for new growth.

To limit shedding, follow these steps:

1. Brush daily with a soft-bristled brush or rubber curry.
2. Run a pumice stone over the coat to pick up dead hair.
3. Bathe more often with an anti-shedding shampoo.
4. Feed a high-quality diet.
5. Supplement with omega-3 fatty acids.

BATHING

Bostons are naturally clean and have very little odor. Although show dogs may require weekly baths to look spiffy in the ring, most pets need them no more than monthly. Some do best on just three or four a year. However, when they decide to play in the mud or roll in something smelly, it's definitely time to reach for the shampoo. A good bath removes surface dirt and dander as it cleans and stimulates the skin. Look for a shampoo made especially for dogs—their hair is more alkaline and their skin more sensitive than ours. Popular formulas include tearless, moisturizing, medicated, and soothing. If your Boston has allergies, select a shampoo without

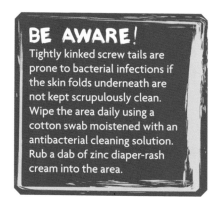

BE AWARE!
Tightly kinked screw tails are prone to bacterial infections if the skin folds underneath are not kept scrupulously clean. Wipe the area daily using a cotton swab moistened with an antibacterial cleaning solution. Rub a dab of zinc diaper-rash cream into the area.

added dyes or fragrances. Baby wipes are great for muddy paws and spot cleaning between baths.

How to Bathe Your Boston

Be sure to assemble all supplies before you begin.

1. Start with a thorough brushing to lift flakes and shed hair. Brush with the hair growth, then against the grain.
2. Place your Boston in the sink or bathtub. Use a rubber mat to prevent slipping.
3. Insert a cotton ball in each ear to keep water from entering the ear canal.
4. Soak the coat completely, using lukewarm water. Include the chest, back, and legs but avoid the head and face.
5. Apply a dab of shampoo between the shoulders and massage into the skin.

A well-groomed Boston Terrier is a joy to behold.

6. Work up a sudsy lather, adding more water and shampoo if needed.
7. Clean the chest, legs, feet, belly, and under the tail.
8. Wash his face with a wet washcloth, but be careful not to get soap or water in his eyes or nose.
9. Rinse completely to clear away all traces of suds that can irritate skin.
10. Wrap your Boston in a fluffy towel and blot dry. Don't let him become chilled!
11. If necessary, use a hair dryer set on cool to finish drying. (A warmer setting can burn your dog's tender skin.)

ANAL SAC CARE

What's that strong, fishy odor? Why is he scooting on the carpet? You may not have been aware of your dog's anal sacs until you notice a painful swelling near his anus. Located on the lower left and right sides of the opening, these sacs secrete an oily substance into the rectum that helps feces pass more easily. The distinctive scent also plays a role in greeting rituals and territorial marking. Passing firm stools during bowel movements puts enough pressure on the sacs to allow them to empty fully. Repeated soft stools or bouts of diarrhea may lead to impaction. Most Bostons never have problems with their anal sacs. However, if you notice an oily discharge or unpleasant smell, then you'll need to empty, or "express," the sacs.

HOW TO CARE FOR THE ANAL SACS

The best time is right before a bath.

1. Place a tissue over the area to absorb any fluid that comes out.
2. With your thumb on one side of the anus (under and slightly behind the sac) and index finger on the other side, gently press in an upward motion to release the fluid.
3. Follow by cleaning the area with shampoo.

If your Boston suffers repeated episodes, he may benefit from a surgical procedure to remove his anal sacs.

DENTAL CARE

Dental problems affect 80 percent of dogs over three years of age, but less than a quarter of owners *ever* brush their pets' teeth. Why is dental care so important? Regular brushing not only removes food particles and bacteria that form plaque but also prevents deposits of crusty yellow-brown tartar. When tartar builds up under the gum line, it leads to gingivitis—red, swollen, and painful gums that bleed easily. If you notice bad breath, blood specks on chew toys, or your Boston has stopped eating, a trip to your veterinarian is in order. Early gum disease is reversible with a professional cleaning and follow-up care at home. If tartar isn't removed from the gum line, it leads to deep pockets that trap debris and then become infected. Periodontal disease results from toxins that break down the supporting structures that hold the teeth in place. When connective tissue and bone are lost, the teeth no longer remain anchored and fall out. This damage is permanent. However, the greatest health risk from periodontal disease occurs when oral bacteria travel via the bloodstream to vital organs. Many disorders of the heart valves, liver, kidneys, and joints can be traced to an untreated dental infection. Brushing your Boston's teeth every day may be the single most effective step you can take to help him feel better and live longer.

DENTAL PRODUCTS

In addition to a toothbrush (or fingerbrush) and toothpaste, the following dental products can enhance your Boston's oral hygiene:

- *Cleaning pads, rinses, and sprays* contain the antiseptic chlorhexidine to kill bacteria. Some are mint flavored to freshen breath.
- *Dental chews and treats* are hard, textured, or crunchy to scrape away tartar and massage gums.
- *Water additives* contain enzymes that inhibit plaque formation.
- *Plaque prevention gel* is a prescription at-home treatment that reduces plaque

and tartar buildup by forming an invisible barrier that prevents bacteria from attaching to teeth.

- *Prescription dental diets* coat the outer surface of kibble with polyphosphates that bind with minerals in the saliva to slow down the progression of plaque to tartar.
- *Dental vaccination* combats a specific bacterium found in a majority of dogs with periodontal disease.

Look for products with the Veterinary Oral Health Council (VOHC) Seal of Acceptance. The VOHC recognizes products that meet preset standards of plaque and tartar reduction.

HOW TO BRUSH YOUR BOSTON'S TEETH

Between four and eight months of age, your Boston will lose his puppy teeth as the adult set emerges. Because Bostons have shorter but wider jaws than most breeds, some of these 42 adult teeth may be crowded, rotated, or misaligned. This close spacing further traps food and bacteria, making regular brushing especially important. Choose a soft-bristled toothbrush (or fingerbrush) made especially for dogs. Select canine toothpaste in a tasty beef or poultry flavor. (Human toothpaste contains ingredients that are harmful if swallowed.)

Inspect your Boston's mouth regularly for dental problems such as plaque and tartar.

Training your Boston to accept brushing requires gentle yet consistent practice, starting as soon as you bring your new puppy home. Keep dental sessions short and pleasant, and offer praise or a small treat after each successful step.

1. Let your puppy examine and sniff the toothbrush.
2. Offer a dab of toothpaste to sniff or lick off your finger.
3. Gently lift his lip and inspect his teeth.
4. Apply toothpaste to one or two front teeth.
5. Rub one or two teeth with a gauze pad.
6. Apply toothpaste to the toothbrush and brush several teeth.
7. Slowly clean more teeth, and be sure to reach the ones in back.
8. Target the gum line when brushing.
9. Return to a previous step if your puppy fusses.
10. Be patient and give plenty of praise when he's a good boy.

EAR CARE

The Boston's naturally erect ears enhance his keen sense of hearing, as the earflaps funnel sound waves to the ear canal and eardrum, then on to the auditory nerve that carries the signals of both hearing and balance to the brain. Unlike breeds with drop ears that cover the canal, the Boston's upright flaps allow easy airflow that helps to keep his ears clean and healthy. All dogs normally host some bacteria and yeast in their ear canals. However, when this balance is disturbed by excessive moisture—from bathing or swimming—an overgrowth can occur. Signs include odor and discharge, along with redness and swelling. Bacterial infections often cause pain, whereas yeast infections result in intense itching. A thorough cleaning with a medicated solution, together with a topical antibiotic ointment, usually resolves a simple infection. Other common problems include excessive wax buildup, allergies, and ear mites. If your Boston is scratching his ears and shaking his head, or you notice a pungent odor, contact your veterinarian. She will identify the organism under a microscope and treat any underlying factors, such as hormonal imbalances or immune deficiencies, that predispose dogs to a variety of ear problems.

HOW TO CLEAN YOUR BOSTON'S EARS

Most cleaning solutions are formulated to not only flush away wax but also change the pH balance of the ear canal from an alkaline environment, which bacteria prefer, to one that is mildly acidic. That's why vinegar and water is a popular home remedy. If the ears are inflamed, however, vinegar can sting and cause further redness and swelling.

To clean the ears properly:

1. Moisten a cotton ball with ear-cleaning solution, or wrap a pre-moistened pad around your finger.
2. Gently grasp the ear and pull it slightly so that you can see inside the ear canal.
3. Wipe the inner surface of the earflap and the visible part of the canal.
4. Use a fresh cotton ball or pad,

To clean the ears properly, use a cotton ball or gauze pad—never a cotton swab, which could damage the ear.

and repeat wiping until it comes out clean.

5. Dry the earflap with a cotton ball.

Never probe into the ear canal with swabs because that just packs the debris deeper and may even injure the eardrum.

HOW TO BRACE YOUR BOSTON'S EARS

Small and folded at birth, the Boston's ears will start to go up by about three months of age. During the teething stage, however, it's normal for the ears to flop forward or curl backward at the tips. The ears go up and down repeatedly before they finally stand on their own, at about eight months. Once the first ear stands, the other will follow shortly. Some owners eagerly await their Bostons' upright ear carriage, but others regret this all-too-quick transition from puppyhood to adulthood.

If a puppy has large or heavy earflaps, the breeder will often brace the ears to help them stand. When supports are placed before six weeks of age, the ears usually go up within a matter of weeks. Beyond the teething stage—four to eight months—they may never fully stand, even with bracing. Whether you choose first-aid tape, nasal strips, or Molefoam to support the earflaps is a personal preference. Keep in mind that plastic products are harmful if swallowed. (Monitor your puppy to make certain that he doesn't accidentally ingest the bracing material.)

If you want to help nature along, try the bracing method described below:

1. Wipe the inside surfaces of the ears with an ear-cleaning pad and allow them to completely dry.
2. Trim each support to fit inside the earflap.
3. Carefully press the support against the natural fold in the ear.
4. Replace the supports whenever they become loose or fall off from the natural oils of the ears.

5. Continue to brace the ears until both ears stand on their own.

For a detailed description of ear bracing, with photographs, see www.boston-terriers.com/ears.htm.

EYE CARE

Have you found that when you touch his whiskers, your Boston instinctively blinks his eyes? In fact, his whiskers help to safeguard his large round eyes by signaling the presence of nearby objects. With his short but wide muzzle, your Boston's eyes are more susceptible to irritants and injuries than those of other breeds. Whenever he plays in tall grass or wooded areas—or roughhouses with his four-legged pals—be sure to inspect his eyes for redness or debris. Flush away dirt and pollen with a mild eye cleaner before they can scratch the corneas. Bostons with dry eyes benefit from a weekly application of artificial tears to bring needed nutrients and moisture to their eyes.

Ear cropping in Bostons is quite rare but is sometimes performed on a show dog whose ears are too wide or long for the conformation ring.

Always contact your veterinarian if you notice excessive tearing, blinking, discharge, or changes in the appearance of the eyes. Bostons are prone to a variety of disorders—from allergies to infections—so never take chances with your Boston's precious eyesight by delaying treatment.

HOW TO CLEAN YOUR BOSTON'S EYES

Routine care consists mainly of wiping off any crusty matter from the corners of the eyes and keeping the surrounding skin clean and dry.

1. Moisten a cotton ball with warm water or eye-cleaning solution, or use a pre-moistened pad.
2. Gently wipe the fur beneath the eye, from the inner to the outer corner. Avoid touching the eye itself.
3. Dry the area thoroughly to prevent tearstains.

HOW TO REMOVE TEARSTAINS

Some Bostons develop tearstains, which are more visible on the white fur that surrounds the eyes. Tearstains form when bacteria and yeast take hold in damp folds of skin—just as they do in moist ear canals. The reddish-brown color comes from pigments found in tears and saliva. The leading factor in staining is the overproduction of tears from allergies or irritation, whereas the other reason is abnormal drainage due to blocked or deformed tear ducts. Tearstains are difficult, if not impossible, to eliminate without an accurate diagnosis of the underlying cause.

Several home remedies promise to fix tearstains, including apple cider vinegar, buttermilk powder, and vitamin and calcium supplements. However, the most successful methods with Bostons are filtering their drinking water and upgrading to higher-quality diets. Antibacterial wipes also aid in fighting local bacteria around the eyes. Check with your veterinarian before using over-the-counter food additives that contain tylosin, an antibiotic given for colitis and diarrhea. Veterinarians have expressed concern about long-term exposure to tylosin and its potential for causing antibiotic resistance.

NAIL CARE

If dogs had the same type of nails—without a "quick"—as humans do, keeping them neatly trimmed would be a much simpler task. The quick is the sensitive core that contains tiny blood vessels and nerve endings that runs the length of the nail. It's visibly pink in light-colored nails but difficult to see in black ones. Accidentally cutting the quick results in bleeding and pain for dogs, leading many owners to put off regular clipping. Nonetheless, nail care is an essential part of grooming. When nails become too long, they are more likely to snag on fabric and carpeting or scratch furniture and flooring.

With his short but wide muzzle, your Boston's eyes are more susceptible to irritants and injuries than those of other breeds.

Long nails also reduce traction, making walking on smooth surfaces a challenge. Rescue organizations see the result of neglect in dogs whose toenails have grown so long that they circle back into the footpads and others who can't stand or walk properly. If you're concerned about clipping your Boston's nails, ask your veterinarian or groomer to show you how. With the right tools and practice, you'll soon be a pro at "pawdicures."

TYPES OF TRIMMING DEVICES

- **Guillotine clipper:** The nail is placed into a stationary ring, and when the handles are squeezed, a sharp blade slides across the ring to slice the nail.
- **Scissors clipper:** The nail is trimmed between two curved or straight scissors-like blades.

• **Rotary grinder:** This tool gradually grinds down the nail, thus offering greater trimming precision.

HOW TO CLIP YOUR BOSTON'S NAILS

Training your Boston to accept nail clipping requires gentle yet consistent practice, starting as soon as you bring your new puppy home. Assemble clippers, nail file, styptic powder, gauze pad, and antibiotic ointment before you begin. If needed, enlist a helper to hold and distract your puppy. Follow each successful step with praise and a small treat.

1. Let your puppy examine and sniff the clippers.
2. Start with a rear paw, which is usually less sensitive, and insert a toenail into the clipper.
3. Trim just a sliver of nail that curves downward.
4. Smooth any rough edges with a nail file.
5. Gradually work up to clipping the nails on one paw, then eventually all the nails—and dewclaws, if present.
6. If the nail starts to bleed, don't panic! Apply pressure with the gauze pad while dabbing the tip with styptic powder. When the bleeding stops, apply antibiotic ointment to the tip of the nail to guard against infection.
7. Inspect your Boston's footpads and trim any excess hair between his toes.
8. If the pads are dry and cracked, rub in a bit of paw wax.

Assemble your nail grooming supplies, including your clippers and nail file, before you start.

HOW TO FIND A PROFESSIONAL GROOMER

PUPPY POINTER

If your puppy protests nail clipping, try a rotary grinder and take off just a bit at a time. Reward good behavior with a favorite treat.

Whether you're short on time or prefer to outsource certain tasks, consider enlisting the services of a professional groomer. Check with your breeder or veterinarian, along with pet-owning friends and family, to locate groomers who have experience with Bostons. Many veterinary clinics offer their clients the added convenience—and safety, in case of an emergency—of onsite grooming. If you have more than one dog, think about a mobile groomer, who brings the salon right to your front door. It's a great way to spruce up your entire pack! The National Dog Groomers Association of America (NDGAA) (www.nationaldoggroomers.com), which offers a variety of workshops, seminars, competitions, and certification testing, provides an online directory of member groomers. Once you've narrowed your choices, call ahead to schedule a tour of the facilities. Ask to meet the groomer who will be working with your dog. Consider the following points when interviewing groomers:

- Is the salon neat and clean, with a minimum of noise and odor?
- Which tasks are included in the basic fee, and which are extra?
- Does the groomer handle pets safely, never leaving them unattended in cage dryers or on tables?
- How much experience does the groomer have?
- Does she understand the grooming needs and health concerns of Boston Terriers?
- Does she attend continuing education classes or grooming conventions, or hold an industry certification, such National Certified Master Groomer from the NDGAA?

HEALTH OF YOUR
BOSTON TERRIER

Whether you're a first-time owner or a veteran of the dog fancy, you'll probably have many questions about the well-being of the little Boston Terrier entrusted to your care. Each pet is different, with his own distinct habits and behaviors. Because he can't describe how he feels, it's vital to be alert to any subtle changes. For example, is your Boston playful and interested in his family and surroundings? Is he sleek and well muscled, neither too fat nor too thin? Are his eyes dark and bright, his coat thick and glossy? Does he have difficulty getting up and lying down?

Many illnesses are fully curable when caught early, whereas others are preventable with a healthy diet, vaccinations against infectious diseases, and spaying or neutering at the appropriate age. Providing regular care at home and veterinary attention, when needed, will enable your Boston to maintain his health from puppyhood through the distinguished graying of old age.

Your veterinarian will help keep your best friend healthy.

FINDING A VETERINARIAN

The veterinarian is a key partner in keeping your best friend well, so choose one before you bring your new puppy home. The breeder may suggest a veterinarian who has experience with brachycephalic (short-nosed) dogs if you're buying locally. Other recommendations may come from dog-owning friends and neighbors, groomers, kennel clubs, and professional associations. To find veterinary hospitals accredited by the American Animal Hospital Association (AAHA), log on to www.healthypet.com. Enter your zip code and the distance you're willing to travel for a list of members with maps to their locations.

After you have narrowed your choices to two or three, schedule appointments to talk with the doctors and tour the areas open to the public. Observe the hospital environment, as well as the staff members. Is this the kind of place you would want to bring your Boston? Is the building clean, bright, and relatively free of unpleasant odors? Are the front desk duties handled efficiently? Do all employees seem to genuinely care about pets? Are the location and hours convenient? Does it offer boarding, grooming, or emergency services? Take your time, and don't be afraid to ask questions. Your Boston's health depends on the care he receives now and throughout his lifetime.

THE ANNUAL WELLNESS EXAM

A stoic fellow who may hide his discomfort under a cheerful demeanor, your Boston should be checked annually by your veterinarian whether or not he shows signs of illness. During this appointment, a technician will weigh your dog, take his temperature, and inspect the fecal sample you brought with you for the presence of parasites or their eggs. Your veterinarian will then discuss the results, decide if vaccines are due, and answer any questions or concerns you might have about your pet's care.

The physical exam involves looking in your Boston's ears, eyes, and mouth; listening to his heart and lungs; inspecting his coat and skin; and palpating his internal organs for any abnormalities. She may also manipulate the kneecaps to check for luxating patellas (slipping kneecaps) and view his gait as he walks across the floor. The exam usually includes a heartworm test, and if needed, a blood panel to serve as a baseline for future comparison. Purchase any medications at this time, renew your dog's license, and request copies of any tests for your records.

VACCINATIONS

Your Boston should be checked annually by his veterinarian, whether or not he shows signs of illness.

Puppies receive temporary immunity to certain infectious illnesses at birth from antibodies—special protein molecules—present in their dam's milk. Because this protection lasts only a few weeks, puppies must develop their own immune response starting at about six weeks of age. Like humans, dogs make an assortment of disease-fighting antibodies after exposure to mild, modified, or killed antigens (substances, such as bacteria or toxins, that stimulate the formation of antibodies). These antibodies, which are specific to their antigen partners, travel throughout the bloodstream, ready to mount an attack if foreign organisms invade the body. While all procedures carry some degree of risk, the safest way to expose puppies to these antigens is by administering a series of controlled vaccinations.

Currently, two vaccination protocols aim to both safely and effectively stamp out deadly diseases: the AAHA Canine Vaccine Guidelines and the W. Jean Dodds DVM Canine Vaccination Protocol. Both agree that adenovirus, distemper, parvovirus, and rabies pose sufficient risk to make them "core" vaccines required of all puppies and adults. The AAHA calls vaccines against kennel cough, leptospirosis, Lyme disease, and parainfluenza "non-core" (optional), whereas Dodds deems them "not recommended." Both view coronavirus and *Giardia* (a single-cell protozoan) as not recommended.

The protocols also differ in the interval between vaccinations. Studies show that certain antibodies remain in a dog's system for up to seven years, so veterinarians are rethinking the benefits versus the risks of yearly boosters. To avoid overvaccination, which has been linked to a variety of adverse reactions, many owners are requesting blood tests—called titer tests—to monitor their dogs' resistance to both distemper and parvovirus. If antibody levels are high based on test results, booster shots may be postponed.

Each of the following illnesses is preventable through vaccination. If your Boston shows symptoms, contact his veterinarian immediately.

CORONAVIRUS

Chiefly seen in puppies less than 12 weeks of age, coronavirus spreads rapidly

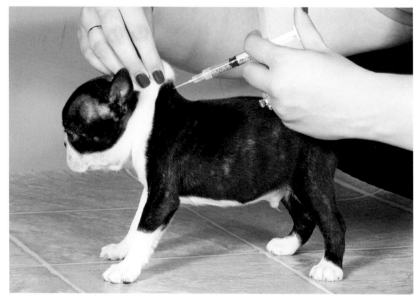

Never take your puppy to canine gathering places until he has received his full set of inoculations.

among the canine population from contact with infected dogs and their feces. The virus enters the digestive tract and grows in the small intestine, causing watery diarrhea and vomiting. Coronavirus has similar symptoms to parvovirus but usually lasts only a few days and is rarely fatal. Treatment is aimed at controlling dehydration by giving fluids, along with medication to stop diarrhea and vomiting. A puppy can shed coronavirus in his feces for weeks or even months, so use a veterinary disinfectant to keep your pet's quarters clean. Never take your puppy to canine gathering places until he has received his full set of inoculations.

DISTEMPER

This highly contagious disease is transmitted through direct or indirect contact with an infected dog. Urine and feces, as well as secretions from the eyes and nose, harbor the virus. Dogs contract distemper from contaminated objects such as bowls, crates, and kennel runs, as well as via air currents. The disease is so widespread that most adult dogs will have been exposed to it at some point in their lifetimes. Signs include fever; nasal discharge, watery eyes, and coughing; and vomiting, diarrhea, and weight loss. In some cases, the virus causes rapid growth of the tough keratin cells on the dog's footpad, resulting in a hardened pad. As it progresses, distemper may attack the nervous system, leading to twitching, convulsions, and partial or complete paralysis. Even if a dog recovers, the damage may be permanent. More than half of all adult dogs who catch the disease die of it, and fewer than one in five puppies survives.

KENNEL COUGH

Known as infectious tracheobronchitis, kennel cough develops from exposure to the bacterium *Bordetella bronchiseptica* or to the viruses parainfluenza and adenovirus. Spread by airborne transfer—when a sick dog coughs—the disease is found mainly in boarding kennels and animal hospitals or at dog shows and dog parks. Puppies and small breeds require special attention because their narrower nasal passages may become obstructed. A home vaporizer helps to relieve congestion. Kennel cough causes inflammation of the upper respiratory tract that leads to harsh, dry coughing fits followed by gagging and retching. Be sure to isolate a sick pet from other animals in the household. Most cases are mild and resolve within several days or weeks. Severe infections may progress to pneumonia, so check with your veterinarian to see whether she advises antibiotics or cough suppressants. Bordetella and parainfluenza are prevented by an intranasal spray, whereas injectable combination vaccines guard against parainfluenza and adenovirus.

Kennel cough is easily transmitted from dog to dog.

LEPTOSPIROSIS

This illness is transmitted by spirochetes (spiral-shaped bacteria) in the urine of infected animals. Rodents, a primary carrier, contaminate a dog's food and water supply. Dogs also pick up leptospirosis through the mucous membranes of the nose and mouth, cuts in the skin, or less frequently, during breeding. Symptoms include vomiting and diarrhea, listlessness, and fever. Your dog may develop sores in his mouth or a brown coating on his tongue. If his liver or kidneys become involved, the whites of his eyes may turn yellow, or he may drink and urinate more than usual. The spirochetes that carry leptospirosis also cause Weil's disease in humans, so take strict sanitary precautions when handling a sick dog. Antibiotics help to fight the infection, but some dogs require hospitalization. Ask your veterinarian whether leptospirosis is a threat in your area. Note that Bostons are particularly sensitive to this vaccine, and some have experienced serious adverse reactions. Unless your puppy is at risk of contracting leptospirosis, consider forgoing this non-core vaccine.

LYME DISEASE

Named for the town of Lyme, Connecticut, where an unusual number of children had been diagnosed with juvenile rheumatoid arthritis (which has similar symptoms), Lyme disease affects both pets and humans alike. Caused by the bacterium *Borrelia burgdorferi*, signs of Lyme disease include lameness and swollen joints, lack of appetite and weight loss, fever, fatigue, and occasionally seizures. As with humans, dogs may or may not show the characteristic round, red bull's-eye rash. Prompt treatment with antibiotics is essential to avoid long-term complications. Unfortunately, symptoms may not appear for months or even years after a tick bite. Although the disease was first identified in 1975, researchers were unable to confirm the mode of transmission—the tiny black-legged (deer) tick—until 1982.

PARVOVIRUS

Highly contagious and often deadly, parvovirus—like coronavirus—is spread through contact with infected dogs and their feces. This robust virus, which can survive for months in soil and on contaminated objects, has been found wherever dogs gather. Parvovirus attacks cells that reproduce rapidly, such as the intestinal lining, bone marrow, lymph nodes, and heart muscle. It can take two forms: enteritis (diarrhea) and myocarditis (heart inflammation). The former causes severe bloody diarrhea, vomiting, and lack of appetite, whereas the latter infects the heart without causing gastrointestinal upsets. Treatment is similar to that for coronavirus: preventing dehydration by giving intravenous fluids, medication to stop diarrhea and vomiting, and antibiotics to fight secondary infections. Recently, veterinarians have experimentally used the human influenza drug, oseltamivir phosphate, to clear up this illness (as well as kennel cough). Because parvovirus is difficult to kill on surfaces, use a veterinary disinfectant to thoroughly sanitize all pet supplies and furnishings.

Parvovirus can survive for months in soil and on contaminated objects.

RABIES

Veterinarians diagnose more than 7,000 cases of rabies annually in the United States. Skunks, raccoons, foxes, and bats, along with dogs and cats, are the main carriers. Present in the saliva, rabies is passed through a bite from an infected animal. Signs usually develop from two weeks to three months after exposure. A rabid dog often undergoes personality changes, becoming withdrawn or irritable. The disease ultimately leads to paralysis and death, but some animals first go through a roaming phase that features aggressive behavior.

To obtain a dog license, most states require vaccination at one- to three-year intervals. However, in 2005, the Rabies Challenge Fund Charitable Trust was founded to determine how long dogs would remain immune to rabies following vaccination. Researchers hope to prove—by measuring serum antibody titers—that protection lasts at least five years after inoculation. The organization believes that reducing the number of vaccinations pets receive over their lifetimes will minimize the potential for a variety of adverse reactions.

PARASITES

Dogs can suffer from two types of parasites: external and internal.

EXTERNAL PARASITES

Whether they jump or crawl their way onto pets, external parasites carry with them a variety of diseases as they bite or burrow into the skin. Be sure to inspect your Boston's fur during regular grooming sessions, and follow your veterinarian's advice on flea and tick control to stop these invaders in their tracks.

Fleas

Is your Boston's skin clean and healthy, with no indication of irritation, flaking, or sores? If he is scratching more than usual—especially on the rump above the tail— flea allergy dermatitis, a reaction to the saliva of biting fleas, might be the culprit. However, you will probably not find parasites on your dog's body. Fleas are remarkable jumpers and spend most of their time off the dog, nestled in bedding, carpets, and grass. Their calling card is the black specks of feces they leave behind in the fur. Fleas not only produce acute itching but can also transmit tapeworms and a host of diseases.

Preventing and eliminating fleas may seem like a never-ending task, but to win the battle you must treat both your dog and his environment. Effective flea products include insecticidal shampoos, dips, powders, foams, and collars. Spot-on treatments, which contain insect growth regulators, are applied to the skin

between the shoulder blades. These not only kill adult fleas but also their eggs and larvae. In addition, once-a-month tablets given orally work by curbing a key step in the flea's reproductive process so that its eggs can't develop and the life cycle is finally broken.

Mites

Four kinds of mites plague our furry friends with itching and scratching as the parasites live out their temporary but tormenting life cycles on a dog's skin. They include ear mites (*Otodectes cynotis*), mange (*Demodex canis*), scabies (*Sarcoptes scabiei*), and walking dandruff (*Cheyletiella yasguri*). Most mites, which come from the family of eight-legged spiders and ticks, affect puppies and elderly dogs or those with weakened immune systems. Treatment depends on identifying the species involved by viewing skin scrapings under a microscope.

The chart on page 74 outlines the signs, modes of transmission, and treatments for mite infestations.

Ticks

The main ticks that feed on dogs are the American and brown dog ticks and the black-legged tick. Ticks are carriers for babesiosis, ehrlichiosis, Lyme disease,

HEALTH OF YOUR BOSTON TERRIER

	Ear Mites	Mange	Scabies	Walking Dandruff
Signs	intense itching and scratching head shaking unpleasant odor waxy reddish-brown or black discharge	intense itching and scratching bald patches and thinning hair on face and forelegs red, scaly skin localized or general forms	intense itching and scratching crusty ear tips hair loss sores	white dandruff on the head, neck, and back mild itching reddish mite visible under magnifying glass
Transmission	direct contact with infected animal	from a dam to her puppies during nursing or other close contact	through the air from animal to animal	direct contact with infected animal and environmental contamination
Treatment	complete ear cleaning pyrethrin or thiabendazole ear medication spot-on imidacloprid/moxidectin or selamectin ivermectin injection*	rotenone ointment and shampoo amitraz dip milbemycin oxime tablets* antibiotics for secondary infections ivermectin injection*	benzoyl peroxide shampoo amitraz or lime-sulfur dip milbemycin oxime tablets* spot-on selamectin antibiotics for secondary infections ivermectin injection*	amitraz or lime-sulfur dip spot-on imidacloprid/moxidectin or selamectin ivermectin injection*
Contagious?	yes, to other pets	no	yes, to other pets and humans	yes, to other pets and humans

*off-label prescription

and Rocky Mountain spotted fever—serious illnesses that affect both dogs and humans. Their bites may also cause skin irritation, sores, and even tick paralysis. Dogs who spend much of their time outdoors pick up ticks in parks and wooded areas. However, birds and other wildlife can carry them right into your own backyard. Be sure to inspect your Boston's coat after a walk in tall grass or underbrush. If you find a tick, grasp it with tweezers as close as possible to the skin and pull straight up with steady pressure, making sure that you've removed the head. Then, disinfect the area with rubbing alcohol and follow with antibiotic ointment. If ticks are a problem in your community, try a spot-on flea-and-tick product or tick-preventing collar for added protection.

INTERNAL PARASITES

Dogs play host to several kinds of internal parasites that reside in the heart and intestines. Some are transmittable to humans, so it's important to have your Boston tested during his annual veterinary checkup. Fortunately, preventive medications and dewormers are available to keep your best friend worm-free.

Dogs who spend much of their time outdoors pick up ticks in parks and wooded areas.

Heartworms

This parasite is responsible for major illness—even death—in dogs. Transmitted by a bite from an infected mosquito, rather than from dog-to-dog contact, heartworms are found throughout the United States and Canada. Heartworms live in the heart, lungs, and large blood vessels, where they can grow up to a foot (.5 m) long. Because adult worms often live for five to seven years within the cardiopulmonary system, they can produce thousands of microscopic worms (microfilaria). When a mosquito bites a dog who has circulating microfilaria, the insect becomes infected and can then transmit the worms to another dog. Both adult and immature heartworms may exist for years without causing symptoms. By the time coughing and difficulty breathing appear, pets are seriously ill. Treatment, which is aimed at killing adult as well as microscopic worms, has many potential complications—even death in cases of especially heavy infestations. Fortunately, heartworms are

preventable with medication. The best age to begin—especially if you live in a region with a large mosquito population—is between 9 and 12 weeks. Your Boston can safely take a once-a-month pill or chewable tablet, which may be given for the duration of mosquito season or year-round as recommended by the American Heartworm Society (AHS).

Other Worms

Other worms that affect dogs include hookworms, roundworms, tapeworms, and whipworms. Worms enter the body as a result of consuming raw meat or fish or from contact with contaminated feces or soil. Fleas are the typical intermediate hosts of tapeworms, whereas the larval stage of hookworms can penetrate the skin. Because puppies may be born with worms or contract them while nursing from an infected dam, they should be wormed at two to three weeks of age and again at five to six weeks. Remember to bring a fresh stool sample to the first veterinary visit. To prescribe the best medication, if needed, your veterinarian must examine the specimen under a microscope to identify the kind of worm involved. She can then choose the safest and most effective wormer to use. When your pet is rid of worms, guard against reinfestation by keeping your yard free of feces. Also, avoid places where strange dogs gather. Worms are less of a problem for adult dogs, who seem to acquire a natural immunity that helps them fight off internal parasites.

SPAYING/NEUTERING

The most important step you can take to ensure your Boston's health—next to obtaining regular vaccinations—is to neuter your puppy before he or she reaches sexual maturity. The surgical procedure in which the sex organs are removed is called castrating in males and spaying in females. Neutering not only prevents the possibility that dogs will sire an unwanted litter or become accidentally pregnant, but it also offers numerous benefits to their physical and emotional well-being. For example, males are less likely to show undesirable traits, such as roaming and marking their territories, following castration. It also lowers the odds of getting testicular cancer, prostate disease, and perianal adenoma—a growth around the anus. Spaying before six months of age nearly eliminates the chances that a female will develop mammary, uterine, or ovarian cancers. It prevents the inconvenience and risk associated with twice-yearly heat cycles as well.

Although neutering is major surgery, it's considered safe—especially for puppies who have smaller reproductive organs. (Neutered dogs can't compete in the show ring but may participate in all obedience and performance events.)

BREED-SPECIFIC PROBLEMS

The Boston Terrier is a hardy and vigorous dog who remains energetic and playful throughout his lifetime. In fact, a life span of 10 to 14 years isn't uncommon. However, breeders, owners, and veterinarians have identified several problems that are significant to anyone considering adding a Boston to their household. Some are hereditary (passed from one generation to another through the genes) or congenital (present at birth). Others occur as a result of infections, exposure to environmental toxins, injuries, or advancing age. The Boston Terrier Club of America (BTCA) has conducted studies that have uncovered the presence of the conditions listed below. The Boston Terrier Health Survey is available online at the Orthopedic Foundation for Animals' (OFA) website (www.offa.org). The Canine Eye Registration Foundation (CERF) (www.vmdb.org) and the OFA maintain registries for diseases that affect Bostons. To help reduce the occurrence

Although neutering is major surgery, it's considered safe— especially for puppies, who have smaller reproductive organs.

of genetic defects, breeders voluntarily submit their dogs' test results for research purposes, as well as for use by individuals who seek to make sound breeding decisions.

In response to these genetic defects—which the BTCA felt were being addressed inadequately—a group of concerned members formed the Health Committee just over a decade ago. A Health Survey, completed in 2001, identified the main hereditary disorders among Boston Terriers. The following year, the committee established the Health Certification program. Designed to educate breeders about relevant ailments, the program also seeks to encourage the selection of healthy animals for breeding purposes.

Club members achieve certification for a given Boston based on annual veterinary examinations. To qualify for a Silver Certificate, a dog must pass his health exam—which includes more than a dozen conditions, in addition to his CERF eye test and OFA patella screening. To earn a Gold Certificate, he must also pass a one-time BAER hearing test. The results are then submitted to the CERF and OFA so that they will be available to researchers and breeders. This voluntary program aims to improve the overall health of Bostons by alerting breeders to the presence of serious genetic defects before they become established—and difficult to eradicate—in their bloodlines.

The Boston Terrier is a hardy and vigorous dog who remains energetic and playful throughout his lifetime.

BRACHYCEPHALIC SYNDROME

The snorts, snuffles, and snoring that distinguish the Boston from other breeds also may signal a more serious airway obstruction called brachycephalic syndrome. The term comes from the Greek, *brachy*, meaning short, and *cephalic*, head. Bulldogs, French Bulldogs, Pekingese, and Pugs are also at risk. Brachycephalic syndrome comprises stenotic nares (constricted nostrils), elongated soft palate (back of the roof of the mouth), and everted laryngeal saccules (small pockets in front of the vocal cords). Dogs can have one or more of these conditions, which may or may not require treatment.

The most common is stenotic nares,

which flap inward during inhalation to close off the nostrils. When dogs have difficulty taking in enough air, they compensate by breathing through their mouths. Their reduced ability to cool themselves through panting means they must forgo heavy exercise, especially in hot or humid weather. Airflow is also diminished when the soft palate extends too far into the back of the mouth. This leads to coughing, gagging, and frothy saliva, which further inflame the throat to cause even greater obstruction. This persistent labored breathing eventually tugs on the laryngeal saccules and everts them (turns them inside out) so that they protrude into the airway.

When brachycephalic syndrome compromises a dog's quality of life, surgery is recommended to widen the nostrils, trim excess palate tissue, and snip off everted saccules. Dogs less than two years of age have the best outcomes from surgery, so this procedure is often performed during neutering.

DEAFNESS

More than 80 breeds are subject to congenital hearing loss. The type found in Bostons is related to the distribution of pigment throughout the coat. The Irish spotting gene, responsible for tuxedo markings, directs pigment cells to specific areas of the embryo before birth. However, another variation—the piebald gene—restricts pigment, thereby yielding full- or half-white faces and/or one or both eyes blue. When migrating pigment cells bypass the vital inner ear, the tiny hairs that transmit sound die off from lack of nourishment. Affected puppies lose their hearing at about three weeks of age. Note that not all Bostons with white faces and/or blue eyes are deaf, but they have two to three times the risk of fully pigmented dogs.

Because a deafness gene has yet to be found, breeders use the Brainstem Auditory Evoked Response (BAER) test to identify and eliminate dogs with unilateral or bilateral hearing loss from their breeding programs. Several tiny electrodes are placed in the scalp to measure the neurological response to computer-generated sounds directed into the ear. The test takes about 15 minutes, requires no sedation, and needs to be performed only once in a dog's lifetime. It confirms whether a puppy is deaf or has normal hearing and is the only way to verify deafness in just one ear. Ask your local kennel club whether it plans to sponsor a BAER clinic if your veterinarian does not have the specialized equipment available.

EPILEPSY

Canine epilepsy, which comprises a group of seizure disorders, usually surfaces between one and five years of age. When no physical abnormalities are found to account for seizures, a dog is said to have primary (idiopathic) epilepsy. This is believed to be hereditary, and several studies funded by the AKC Canine Health Foundation, National Institutes of Health, Canine Epilepsy Project, and others seek to locate the genes responsible and ultimately develop a DNA screening test. Such a tool would allow breeders to eliminate affected dogs, as well as carriers of the defective gene, from their bloodlines.

Not all Bostons with white faces and/or blue eyes are deaf, but they have two to three times the risk of fully pigmented dogs.

Secondary epilepsy, on the other hand, results from infections, kidney or liver failure, low blood sugar or thyroid levels, or tumors that impact critical areas of the brain. (Brachycephalic breeds are at a significantly greater risk of developing brain tumors than is the general canine population, so bring any neurological symptoms to your veterinarian's attention without delay.) Vitamin and mineral deficiencies, as well as exposure to the preservatives BHA, BHT, and ethoxyquin, have also been implicated. The limited-ingredient duck-and-potato food and the Glutamate and Aspartate Restricted Diet (GARD) have benefited some Bostons.

Epilepsy is a chronic condition that requires close partnership between you and your veterinarian. Underlying problems, which may be treatable, must be ruled out by blood panels and image studies before the drugs, phenobarbital, potassium bromide, or gabapentin are given to control seizure activity.

HEMIVERTEBRAE

Imagine stringing cylindrical beads on a cord but in the midst of the row inserting a triangle instead. It throws the straight line out of kilter, which is similar to what happens to the spine of a dog with hemivertebrae. This congenital malformation with a genetic basis develops in the womb, when the two halves of a vertebra fail to completely fuse. The distorted vertebra appears wedge-shaped from the side and resembles a butterfly from above. Breeds with corkscrew tails, including Bulldogs, French Bulldogs, and Pugs, are at greatest risk. In fact, the screw tail's curvature is a form of hemivertebrae. When the tail or only a single vertebra are involved, most dogs show no symptoms and the condition may be uncovered accidentally. However, if multiple hemivertebrae compress the spinal cord, puppies may experience back pain, loss of bladder and bowel control, or weakness and paralysis of their hind legs. At this point, surgery is the only option to relieve the constriction.

HEREDITARY CATARACTS

Bostons are prone to more than 20 eye disorders, but one of the most serious is a cataract—an opacity of the lens of the eye. The lens, which lies behind the iris, is clear in order to focus visual images on the retina. When a cataract obscures the lens, light no longer reaches the retina and eyesight diminishes. Without surgery to remove the cataract and replace the diseased lens with an artificial one, a dog can become totally blind.

Cataracts form as a result of diabetes, nutritional deficiencies, and trauma, but the most likely cause is heredity. At least 70 breeds carry genes for cataracts. Bostons are subject to two distinct types: early-onset and late-onset hereditary cataracts. Also called juvenile cataracts, early-onset cataracts progress quickly and always affect both eyes. They can be seen in puppies as young as 8 to 12 weeks and may lead to total blindness in as little as a year. However, late-onset

If your Boston appears unusually lethargic or unwell, take him to his veterinarian.

cataracts advance slowly once they emerge at three to six years of age. This variety is neither related to the early-onset form nor to cataracts acquired in old age.

A major breakthrough took place in 2006 in the United Kingdom, when the Animal Health Trust identified the gene responsible for juvenile cataracts in Bostons. Breeders now have access to a DNA test that detects carriers so that one day this defect may be eliminated from the canine population.

Patellar luxation, or slipping kneecaps, makes it difficult for a Boston to engage in everyday activities, like stair climbing.

LUXATING PATELLAS

Characterized by limping, pain, and difficulty straightening the hind leg, luxating patellas—slipping kneecaps—are more prevalent in small breeds than large ones. Several factors predispose Bostons to knee problems, such as weak ligaments that support the kneecap, poor alignment of muscles and tendons, and a too-shallow groove in the femur (thighbone). Veterinarians diagnose the disorder by manipulating the kneecap and viewing X-rays to detect arthritic changes.

Luxating patellas are graded from one to four, based on the severity of the dislocation. Grade 1 means the kneecap slips out of position only when manipulated, whereas Grade 4 remains constantly dislocated even with the hind leg fully extended. Treatment involves crate rest, controlled exercise on leash, pain medication, and weight reduction, if needed. Surgery to deepen the femoral groove has been quite successful, especially in young dogs or in those with persistent lameness.

MAST CELL TUMOR

Whenever you brush your dog's coat, make certain to inspect his skin for any unusual lumps or bumps. Bostons are prone to benign growths, as well as to potentially malignant mast cell tumors. The former targets dogs under age 3, whereas the latter aims at those between ages 9 and 11. Both types of growths

Whenever you brush your dog's coat, make certain to inspect his skin for any unusual lumps or bumps.

look nearly identical—raised, red, hairless, ulcerated nodules. The only way to tell the difference is by extracting cells with a syringe and examining them under a microscope.

Mast cells, born in the bone marrow and critical to the immune system, contain microscopic granules that store histamine and heparin (a blood thinner). When confronted by allergens or parasites, mast cells discharge their toxic payload to stamp out the invaders. Unfortunately, when tumors are manipulated during an exam or in surgery, they can spontaneously release massive amounts of these chemicals, resulting in hives, gastric ulcers, internal bleeding, or even shock and death.

Mast cell tumors—which are more prevalent in the short-nosed breeds—make up 20 percent of all skin tumors but are also found in the liver, spleen, and bone marrow. Tumors are graded between I and III (whether their cellular structure suggests cancer) and staged from 0 to IV (how far it has spread). Lower grades and stages have better prognoses than if tumors are situated on the muzzle, nail bed, genital area, or internal organs.

The standard treatment is "wide excision"—surgically removing 2 to 3 centimeters of healthy tissue in all directions. However, radiation is an option when the nodule can't be cleanly removed, such as on a toe. Other remedies include chemotherapy and steroids that shrink the number of mast cells within the tumor. In 2009, the U.S. Food and Drug Administration (FDA) approved the first medicine specifically designed to treat canine cancer, toceranib phosphate, and a year later, masitinib. These drugs not only block the spread of mast cell tumors but may also be less toxic than older therapies because they target specific molecules on the mast cells themselves.

PUPPY POINTER

If your puppy has difficulty swallowing pills, have his prescription filled at a compounding pharmacy. The pharmacist can reformulate the medicine as a chewable tablet or flavored liquid for easy dosing.

OTHER PROBLEMS

Other problems include cleft palate, in which the roof of the mouth fails to fully fuse before birth; cherry eye, the prolapse of the third eyelid and its tear-producing gland; corneal ulcer, the loss of the outermost layer of the cornea due to dry eye, infection, or injury; cryptorchidism, one or both testicles retained within the abdomen; glial tumors, a type of brain tumor that poses an increased risk for brachycephalic breeds; hip dysplasia, the abnormal development of the ball-and-socket joint leading to osteoarthritis; hypothyroidism, an abnormally low production of thyroid hormones; and megaesophagus, an enlarged esophagus that lacks adequate muscular contractions to transport food to the stomach.

GENERAL ILLNESSES

The previous section discussed illnesses that are known to occur in Boston Terriers. However, a variety of ailments affect dogs of all breeds. For more in-depth information about these and other diseases, invest in a comprehensive health manual or refer to a reliable online reference.

ALLERGIES

If your Boston is caught in a vicious cycle of itching and scratching, a reaction to one or more substances in his environment is likely to blame. Allergies, which typically appear between one and three years of age, develop when the immune system detects an allergen and produces antibodies that attach to mast cells in the skin. The mast cells then release histamine, which causes intense itching, redness, rashes, and—if not resolved—secondary bacterial and yeast infections. Most canine allergies show up in the skin, whether they are due to inhaled (pollen, mold, dust mites), ingested (protein, grains), or contacted (fabrics, carpets, grasses) substances.

The best way to help an allergic pet is to avoid whatever causes the immune system to overreact. Weekly shampoos and topical creams provide temporary relief from the itch–scratch cycle. Medications

Inhaled allergens, such as pollen, can affect a dog's skin.

Some home-cooked diets can significantly decrease tummy upset in Bostons.

and supplements for treating allergies include antihistamines, corticosteroids, cyclosporine, probiotic food additives, and omega-3 fatty acids. Allergy shots benefit a majority of dogs but are a time-consuming and costly option that takes up to a year for full effect. If skin problems persist, contact the American College of Veterinary Dermatology (ACVD) (www.acvd.org) for a list of specialists in your area.

DIARRHEA

Most dogs have diarrhea—watery, soft, or frequent stools—at some point in their lives. Factors that lead to diarrhea include those related to food (allergies, changes in diet, raiding the garbage), parasites (Coccidia, cryptosporidiosis, *Giardia*, worms), infections (corona- and parvovirus, distemper, *E. coli*, *Salmonella*), excitement or stress, and intestinal blockages.

Home care is aimed at easing inflammation by resting the digestive tract. Withhold food (but not water) for the first 12 to 24 hours. Over the next few days, feed a bland diet of rice with lean beef or chicken. Give a teaspoon of the pink bismuth anti-diarrhea liquid medication every three to four hours. Also, add a tablespoon of plain canned pumpkin (not pie filling) to your dog's food. The fiber in pumpkin relieves both diarrhea and constipation.

Call your veterinarian if your dog has a fever, pain, or bloating or the diarrhea lasts more than a day or two. Dehydration is a serious state that occurs when more fluids are excreted than are taken in. Delay in replacing these lost fluids, either orally or intravenously, can be deadly—especially for puppies. Also, take a fresh stool sample with you so that your veterinarian can identify any parasites that may be present.

FLATULENCE

Whether it routinely clears the room or occasionally offends, flatulence is a common complaint that can be reduced or eliminated altogether. The two main causes are swallowing air during eating and the process of breaking down certain foods by bacteria in the large intestine. Switching to an anti-gulping bowl can reduce the gas produced from swallowing air, which happens when dogs eat too quickly. Smaller, more frequent meals also help. On the other hand—as many Boston owners can attest—gas produced in the colon can be quite odorous. It occurs when dogs overeat, consume high-fiber diets, or ingest specific foods that disagree with them.

Finding the right foods that minimize flatulence involves trial and error because each dog has his own sensitivities. Problem ingredients include dairy, fruit, grains, beans and legumes, and sometimes poultry. Home-cooked, raw, grain-free, and low-residue diets have significantly decreased bouts of flatulence. And if all else fails, take your dog for a walk after meals so that most of the gases are expelled outdoors.

HIVES

One minute he's fine and the next he's sprouted a patchwork of marble-size lumps. Or perhaps his muzzle and eyes have become itchy and puffy. Hives (urticaria) and facial swelling (angioedema) come on rapidly (within 30 minutes) after exposure to an allergen. Because they develop quickly, try to determine what has changed in the household. Has your Boston eaten a new food or treat? Been stung by a bee? Come into contact with household or lawn chemicals? Even heat and sunlight can cause an outbreak.

Hives usually go away on their own within 24 hours. In the meantime, bathe your dog in cool water using a mild shampoo. This not only relieves itching but also removes any harmful substances from the coat. Owners whose dogs have experienced repeated episodes keep the antihistamine diphenhydramine on hand for prompt administration. The usual dosage is 1 milligram per pound (.5 kg) of body weight. If hives or facial swelling last more than a day or two, contact your veterinarian to find the possible trigger.

RINGWORM

A family of fungi that live in hair follicles—not a worm at all—causes the round bald patches known as ringworm. Lesions are scaly, with small pustules in the center, but may or may not be red and itchy. The main sites are the face, ears, feet, and tail. Dogs contract ringworm through direct contact with infected animals (or humans) or indirectly from spore-covered supplies and furnishings. Spores that land in soil can spread ringworm for up to 18 months.

Several skin disorders mimic ringworm, such as mange and scabies, so it's important to have your veterinarian accurately identify the specific microorganism involved. Should your Boston be diagnosed with ringworm, wear gloves during handling, and isolate him from children and other pets in the household. Treatment includes topical anti-fungal cream, shampoo, or dips, or oral medication until the lesions have healed. To guard against a second outbreak, clean all equipment and hard surfaces with a veterinary disinfectant. Wash bedding in hot water, and vacuum carpets and upholstery daily.

VOMITING

Whereas diarrhea results from inflammation of the intestines, vomiting is due to irritation of the stomach itself. Both conditions go hand in hand. As with diarrhea, vomiting may be caused by food-related factors, parasites, or infections, as well as liver, pancreatic, or kidney disease. Pay special attention if your dog is taking nonsteroidal anti-inflammatory drugs (NSAIDs) for pain relief because these can cause stomach ulcers and bleeding. For isolated episodes of vomiting, allow the digestive tract to rest overnight. Withhold food and water until six hours after vomiting has stopped. Then, follow the feeding plan for relieving diarrhea. Contact your veterinarian if your dog has a fever, bloody vomit, pain or bloating, or you suspect that he may have eaten something toxic.

ALTERNATIVE THERAPIES

East meets West in today's veterinary practices as alternative therapies—like acupuncture, chiropractic, and herbal remedies—take their place next to conventional techniques to keep pets in optimal health. This holistic method combines the strengths of Western medicine, such as antibiotics for infectious diseases, with the benefits of a more comprehensive approach to wellness. Veterinarians who take an integrative approach delve deeper—beyond immediate symptoms—to discover which behavioral, dietary, and environmental factors might contribute to the underlying illness. To locate a veterinarian certified in holistic medicine, contact the American Holistic Veterinary Medical Association (AHVMA) (www.ahvma.org).

- **Acupuncture:** Based on the Traditional Chinese Medicine concept of *qi*—the life force that travels throughout the body—acupuncture places thin needles at specific blockage points to restore the flow of energy to affected areas. Most

Traditional Chinese Medicine is based on the concept of balancing *qi*, the life force that travels throughout the body.

pets readily accept acupuncture, which induces relaxation as it strengthens the immune system and alleviates the pain of arthritis, back disorders, and muscle and nerve problems.

- **Chiropractic:** Specific manipulations and adjustments to spinal vertebrae not only ease pain but also improve blood flow to internal organs.
- **Herbal remedies:** This ancient system of medicine uses whole plants and extracts, both orally and in the form of aromatherapy, to treat an array of conditions. A promising weapon in the battle against mast cell tumors and other cancers is Neoplasene, a plant-derived alkaloid from the herb bloodroot, which is given as a pill, injected, or applied directly to the skin. Because herbs contain active ingredients that may interfere with prescription drugs, always check with your veterinarian before administering plant-based remedies.

SENIOR DOGS

Advances in veterinary medicine—especially in the prevention and treatment of diseases, progress in nutritional research, and the rise of knowledgeable pet owners—allow dogs to live longer and healthier lives than ever before. Responsible breeding practices aimed at eliminating hereditary defects have also contributed to an increased quality of life for today's Boston Terrier. However, to fully understand aging, it's important to appreciate what the process is—and isn't. Aging is neither a disease, nor must it be accompanied by disease.

A dog's body comprises myriad cells that receive nourishment from oxygen and other substances carried by the bloodstream. When old cells die off, new ones generate to take their places. Over time, cells die off faster than they can be replaced. Improper nutrition, lack of exercise, and environmental factors also add to the progressive changes associated with aging. By the time your Boston celebrates his seventh or eighth birthday, you'll notice that he has less energy for those rollicking BT 500s. He may sleep longer and snore louder than usual or

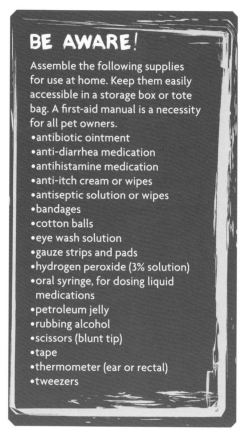

BE AWARE!

Assemble the following supplies for use at home. Keep them easily accessible in a storage box or tote bag. A first-aid manual is a necessity for all pet owners.
- antibiotic ointment
- anti-diarrhea medication
- antihistamine medication
- anti-itch cream or wipes
- antiseptic solution or wipes
- bandages
- cotton balls
- eye wash solution
- gauze strips and pads
- hydrogen peroxide (3% solution)
- oral syringe, for dosing liquid medications
- petroleum jelly
- rubbing alcohol
- scissors (blunt tip)
- tape
- thermometer (ear or rectal)
- tweezers

There are many things you can do to make your senior Boston more comfortable, including treating him with unconditional love and kindness.

complain when suddenly roused. His joints may feel stiff and painful, especially in chilly weather. (Remember that Bostons are an indoor breed—they can't tolerate excessive heat or cold.) Yet there are many steps you can take to delay aging, as well as to make your pet more comfortable.

First, regular checkups will help to spot potential problems while the underlying condition is still easily treatable. Limit exposure to chemicals, such as topical insecticides and lawn pesticides, and vaccinate based on the likelihood of coming into contact with contagious microorganisms. Depending on where you live and your dog's activities, certain boosters may be unnecessary. Dental care also plays a vital role in preventing damage to the heart, kidneys, and liver from oral bacteria that spread throughout the body. Finally, to help your Boston Terrier not only survive but also thrive during his Golden Years, always return his lifetime of unconditional love with kindness, patience, and understanding.

TRAINING YOUR BOSTON TERRIER

erhaps the best-kept secret about Boston Terriers is that they are smart, trainable, and eager to please. This cheerful fellow thrives on human interaction and quickly catches on to whatever is asked of him. Bostons are capable of a large vocabulary but become bored with endless repetition of commands. When teaching a new skill, always maintain an upbeat attitude and follow any successful achievement with enthusiastic praise and a small reward. Bostons try hard to do what is expected of them, but they wilt under a harsh tone of voice or physical correction. Positive training—acknowledging and rewarding desired behavior—is the best way to teach this sensitive breed. Turn training sessions into a game and there is no limit to what you and your Boston can accomplish.

Boston Terriers are smart, trainable, and eager to please.

WHY TRAIN YOUR BOSTON?

One of the most enjoyable aspects of dog ownership is the bond that forms as you and your dog learn to communicate as a team through the process of training. A trained dog is happier and more self-confident than one left to his own devices. He understands his boundaries and status within the family, and he knows what is acceptable so that he doesn't have to guess which action might bring a rebuke. Because Bostons naturally are a social breed—the center of attention—it's especially important that they are taught manners around people and other pets. No one likes a dog who makes a pest of himself by barking uncontrollably, lunging on his leash, or jumping up on household visitors. Note that tolerating rudeness just because a puppy is cute will result in an undisciplined adult who is no longer welcome in your friends' homes or public places. So why train your Boston? It's the only way to turn a rambunctious puppy into an American Gentleman.

POSITIVE TRAINING

Gone are the days of choke-chain collars, corrective jerks, stern commands, and physical discipline. Today, professional trainers and pet owners alike rely on positive training to shape their dogs' behavior. This method rewards a dog for performing correctly, rather than punishing him for making a mistake. No dog should be forced to respond out of fear; training should be a fun activity for both

human and canine participants.

To use positive training, choose a command, such as *sit*, which is easy for most Bostons to master. As soon as he squats into position, immediately praise and give a small reward. Bostons are highly motivated by food, but some prefer a favorite toy or game instead. One owner who competes in agility tosses a ball when her Boston has performed a clean run through the dozen weave poles. If you choose food, make certain that it's small (pea size) and chewable so that you don't have to wait while he crunches a full-size biscuit. After your dog has mastered a particular command, gradually withdraw treats the majority of the time but continue to offer praise and petting.

Positive training involves rewarding your dog with praise and treats for performing a command correctly.

To learn more about positive training or to find instructors who use dog-friendly techniques, contact the Association of Pet Dog Trainers (APDT). Log on to its website at www.apdt.com and enter your zip code and the distance you're willing to travel for a list of certified trainers in your area.

SOCIALIZATION

Boston enthusiasts are a sociable group that stands ready to welcome like-minded newcomers to the fold. From local meet-ups to distant getaways, owners and their pets gather for shared camaraderie and activities. Canine participants, of course, are expected to be polite in such company. However, proper manners come not only from training but also through early socialization. An oft-overlooked duty of puppy rearing is socialization—exposing him to a variety of people, pets, and places, and sights, smells, and sounds. Puppies are most receptive to new experiences between three weeks and three months of age.

HOW TO SOCIALIZE

The breeder will have begun socializing your puppy before he leaves his dam and littermates, but it's important to continue to provide new experiences every day. For example, take your Boston to shops, offices, or outdoor markets where he can interact with people of all ages, genders, and ethnic backgrounds.

Have the neighborhood children gently pet and play with him. Let him walk on different surfaces, explore new scents, and interact with other pets. Expose him to household sounds—ringing telephone, television, music, appliances. Or play a socialization CD that mimics children's voices, thunderstorms, vehicles, and other noises he is likely to encounter. Puppy kindergarten classes are an ideal venue for socialization in a safe and controlled environment. Be sure to allow your puppy to progress at his own pace—never rush or overwhelm him with too much stimulation—and make certain that he is happy and relaxed throughout the exercise. End each new adventure on a positive note, with a favorite toy or treat.

VACCINATIONS AND SOCIALIZATION

A valid concern with early socialization is whether it's safe to take a puppy to new locations before he has received his full set of inoculations. Not long ago, owners were warned to confine puppies to the house and backyard until vaccination was complete. However, the American Veterinary Society of Animal Behavior (AVSAB) believes that early socialization, including puppy classes, is so vital to overall fitness that the benefits now outweigh the risks. Vaccines have improved as well, with doses given at 6, 9, and 12 weeks as effective as the older set that was completed at 18 weeks. It's still necessary to avoid places like dog parks, but structured classes that follow sanitary precautions are considered safe. In fact, the AVSAB finds that the behaviors associated with lack of socialization—fear, avoidance, and aggression—pose a much greater risk than the potential of contracting an illness.

CRATE TRAINING

Resembling the hidden dens of their wild ancestors, crates offer a sense of security to modern-day canines. By confining puppies to their instinctive nesting areas, crates aid in the task of housetraining while they minimize chewing and other destructive behaviors. Crates shield inquisitive puppies from household hazards and provide safe havens where dogs can relax and sleep undisturbed. When traveling by car, they protect pets from injury or escape in the event of an accident, and they keep them

To socialize your Boston, let him interact with other pets.

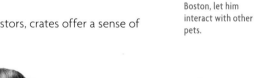

confined in hotel rooms when their owners go out on the town. Crates also serve as "sick bays" for Bostons who must temporarily limit their activities for medical reasons. In short, crates are an indispensable means of safeguarding pets in any number of unpredictable circumstances.

CRATE SIZE

Crates should be just large enough to stand up, turn around, and lie down. Those that are too large defeat their purpose for housetraining because puppies can eliminate at one end while still keeping their bed clean. Select a crate based on your Boston's anticipated adult size. Airline-style cabins and fold-down wire crates work equally well, but mesh, fabric, and wicker may be too flimsy to withstand energetic and teething puppies. If a wire crate is too drafty, use a fabric crate cover. You'll often see custom-made covers at dog shows, personalized with the breeder's kennel name or logo. A small crate (24" L × 18" W × 21" H [61 cm L

Introduce your Boston to the crate slowly, first allowing him to check it out on his own.

× 45.5 cm W × 53.5 cm H]) is best for Bostons under 25 pounds (11 kg), whereas a medium crate (30" L × 21" W × 24" H [76 cm L × 53.5 cm W × 61 cm H]) suits those up to 40 pounds (18 kg). You can section off a smaller area for your puppy with an adjustable divider available from the crate manufacturer.

HOW TO CRATE TRAIN

1. Set up the crate in a people-oriented area, such as the kitchen or family room. Line the bottom with washable towels to make a comfortable bed.
2. To coax your Boston to enter, leave the door open and put a favorite toy or treat inside.
3. Use a command word like "kennel!" to instruct your puppy to enter the crate.
4. When he goes inside, praise "Yes!" or "Good dog!" and give a treat.
5. Once he confidently goes in and out, close the door for a minute or two. If he behaves, open the door and praise him. Don't automatically let him out if he barks or whines—just ignore him until he settles down.
6. Gradually lengthen the time your Boston stays in his crate. A general rule is one hour for every month in age but no more than five to six hours for an adult. If you work full time, consider hiring a sitter to walk him at midday or enroll him in doggy day care a few times per week.
7. Remove his collar and make certain that he has fully eliminated before an extended crate stay.
8. Provide safe, entertaining toys, such as hard rubber toys stuffed with cheese or peanut butter.
   Respect your Boston's need for privacy, and *never* use the crate for punishment.

HOUSETRAINING

The first task your Boston must learn is the proper place to eliminate. Some owners put down indoor piddle pads, but it's less confusing when pets go outdoors right from the start.

HOW TO HOUSETRAIN

1. As soon as you bring your new puppy home, take him to the spot to which you want him to return. This is his designated potty area. Watch him like a hawk, and be ready to move whenever he signals that he needs to go out.
2. Have his leash handy and carry him to the location.
3. Choose a special word—one that you're not embarrassed to say in public— and use it each time you want your puppy to eliminate.
4. Praise lavishly and offer a small treat when he performs.

It's important to respond to your puppy's cues, even if you don't think he needs to go. This helps to reinforce his attempts to alert you. Most Bostons quickly grasp the concept of housetraining, but some have difficulty letting their owners know when they have to potty. It's important to decode his signals—sniffing, circling, or whining—and take immediate action. Be patient with your Boston— some pick up housetraining more quickly than others, but by six months to a year of age your dog should be accident-free.

BE CONSISTENT

Always feed and water at the same times each day—even on weekends—and follow a regular schedule of walks. Also, take your puppy outside as soon as he awakens in the morning, after meals, following naps and play sessions, and just before bedtime. You might have to take him out during the night as well until he develops greater control of his bladder and bowels. A puppy often needs to go out every hour or two, so don't disregard his warnings or housetraining will be that much more difficult.

To prevent housetraining accidents, feed and water your Boston at the same times each day.

CRATE YOUR PUPPY

Because dogs by nature prefer to keep their quarters clean, crating lets you determine when, as well as where, your Boston will eliminate. Set up his crate where you can watch for signs that he needs to go out. Take him to the same spot each time, and praise enthusiastically when he performs. If he doesn't go, put him back in his crate and try again every 15 minutes until . . . success!

ACCIDENTS

Of course, all puppies have occasional accidents, so don't scold your Boston unless you catch him in the act. Because he has a short memory, he won't be able to associate your displeasure with his mistake. To prevent future soiling, use an enzyme-based stain remover to clean the spot and eliminate all traces of odor. Bostons may have a reputation for being difficult to housetrain, but they actually master this fundamental concept easily and quickly.

HOUSETRAINING TIPS

- Establish a regular feeding and walking schedule.
- Don't give water closer than two or three hours before bedtime.
- Watch your puppy carefully and take him out immediately when he signals that he needs to go.
- Praise lavishly when he performs correctly.
- When you're not with him, keep him confined in a secure area until he has proved that he can be trusted.
- Never give an untrained puppy the run of the house.
- Give the same command each time he eliminates.
- Never scold him unless you catch him in the act, and never use harsh punishment under any circumstances.
- If your adult (already trained) dog starts to soil in the house, have him thoroughly checked by your veterinarian for any underlying health problems.

BASIC COMMANDS

Puppies differ in their attention spans and ability to focus, but most are ready for basic commands by 10 to 12 weeks of age. Don't expect perfect performance at this point, however. Bostons don't settle down and develop the concentration needed for more advanced obedience skills until their first or second birthday.

When you give a command, speak in a normal tone of voice and don't whisper or shout. Bostons are quite sensitive to loud or stern tones and shut down when faced with their owners' wrath. Give the instruction once; then wait a few seconds for your puppy to obey. When he correctly performs, offer a small treat and praise with a heartfelt "Yes!" or "Good dog!"

To avoid confusing your puppy with multiple demands, work on a single exercise at a time. Always use the same word and avoid complicated phrases. Keep sessions short—10 to 15 minutes at most. Because Bostons become easily distracted, work indoors or in a confined area until your dog has mastered the command. Later, move to more stimulating environments to further refine his skills. Plan each lesson in advance, and end on a positive note with a fun trick that your puppy can do well. And be sure to maintain a sense of humor—you'll discover that your Boston has one as well.

When you're not with your unhousetrained Boston, keep him confined in a secure area until he has proved that he is trustworthy.

SIT

This is the easiest command for most puppies to learn and the first step in mastering the more advanced *come, stay, down,* and *heel*. Success here breeds both self-confidence and self-control. *Sit* provides an acceptable alternative to unwanted behaviors, like jumping up on visitors, and it gives your puppy guidance on what to do in unfamiliar situations. Perhaps the greatest benefit is the breakthrough that occurs when your puppy learns how to sift through the gibberish of human conversation and pick out those words meant just for him. This ability to communicate with your dog—verbally and nonverbally—and his capacity to understand forms the basis of every other activity in which the two of you choose to participate.

Teaching *Sit*

1. Stand or kneel in front of your Boston so that you are facing each other. Show him the treat.

The *sit* is the easiest command for most Bostons to learn.

2. Hold the treat in front of his nose and move it up, in an arcing motion, over his head.
3. Say "Sit!"
4. When he looks up to follow the treat, he will shift his weight onto his haunches.
5. Immediately praise "Yes!" or "Good dog!" and give the treat.
6. If he backs up instead of sitting, place him in a corner or have a partner kneel behind him. If he jumps up for the treat, hold it closer to his head.
7. Practice the command a few more times, offering the treat only intermittently.
8. Give the verbal cue without the hand signal, and vice versa, so that your puppy learns both forms of the command.
9. Reinforce the command by periodically having him sit before you put down his dinner bowl or begin a play session.
10. If you plan to compete in formal

obedience, be sure that your Boston sits straight and doesn't lean sideways on one hip. (Crooked *sits* will result in points off in competition.)

Never push down on your Boston's hips when teaching *sit*. This not only causes pain but also contributes to joint problems in susceptible dogs.

COME

For safety's sake, *come* is the most important command your Boston will learn. Whether he breaks free from his leash or escapes under the backyard fence, he absolutely *must* come back to you when you call him. The best way to teach *come* is to turn it into a game. Have friends sit in a circle and take turns calling the puppy to them. Each person should offer a treat when he comes running. Reinforce *come* by using the command when you put down your Boston's dinner bowl or pick up his leash. Always make certain that something delightful awaits your puppy when he comes to you—never call him for an unpleasant chore, like nail clipping, and never scold or discipline him when he comes or he may not be willing to do so when it matters most.

Teaching *Come*

1. Stand in front of your Boston, facing him, and give the *sit* command. Reward him.
2. Step back two or three paces and say "Come!"
3. Open your arms or pat your legs to encourage him.
4. When he starts moving toward you, praise "Yes!" Give the treat when he is in front of you.
5. When he comes reliably indoors, move to a fenced-in area outdoors where he faces greater distractions.

   Never allow your Boston off leash unless he always responds promptly to your command. This breed can take off in a heartbeat and is difficult to capture when he disobeys!

DOWN

This command, in which your puppy lies down on cue, comes in handy when you want him to remain in one place for extended periods of time. *Down* also teaches self-control in distracting situations, such as at the dog park or veterinarian's office. Some Bostons dislike having to lie down because they feel vulnerable in submissive positions. However, with practice and a few tasty treats for good measure, *down* will soon be one of your dog's favorite skills.

Teaching *Down*

1. Start with your Boston facing you in the *sit* position. Show him the treat.
2. Hold the treat in front of his nose and move it down between his front paws toward the floor.
3. Say "Down!"
4. When he follows the treat, he will lower his head and front legs to a prone position.
5. Immediately praise "Yes!" and give the treat.
6. Alternate the verbal cue with the hand signal so that your puppy learns both forms of the command.

The *down* comes in handy when you want your dog to remain in one place for an extended period.

Never pull your Boston's front legs into position or push down on his back, which could physically harm him.

STAY

After your puppy has learned to sit or lie down on command, you can teach him to stay—remain in one spot until you release him. This skill not only prevents your Boston from darting out an open door but may also save his life if you need to fetch him from a potentially dangerous situation.

Teaching *Stay*

1. Stand next to your Boston, facing forward, and give the *sit* or *down* command. Reward him.
2. Place your hand in front of his face, fingers downward and palm toward him, and say "Stay!"
3. Step away two or three paces and stop. Pause for a moment.
4. Return to his side. Praise "Yes!" and give the treat.
5. Say the release phrase, such as an enthusiastic "All done!" to let him know that it's okay to move.
6. To achieve the type of *sit-stay* or *down-stay* required in the obedience ring, gradually increase the distance you move away from your dog and the length of time he must wait in position. Should he move during the *stay*, return to the previous level until he remains still.

Never allow your Boston to free himself from a *stay* by forgetting to give the release command.

HEEL (WALK NICELY ON LEASH)

No breed looks sharper when out for a walk than the Boston Terrier. Whether he sports a matching collar-and-leash set or a handsome sweater, all eyes follow the "man in black" (and white). Because he attracts so much attention, he must learn to walk nicely on his leash—without forging ahead, pulling, or lagging behind. This is accomplished with daily practice using only positive training methods.

To teach this command, select a flat buckle or quick-release collar that allows you to fit one or two fingers between his neck and the collar. If he tends to slip out of a standard collar, try a martingale collar that tightens to prevent escape but won't choke him. Choke-chain collars can hurt the trachea if repeatedly jerked, and even flat collars may cause harm when dogs pull hard against them. Until your Boston learns to walk on a loose lead, consider having him wear a harness to distribute the pulling forces across his chest and shoulders rather than against his neck. (Never allow him to pull so hard that he injures himself.) Add a flat webbed cotton or nylon leash and you're ready to go!

Teach your Boston to walk nicely on leash without forging ahead, pulling, or lagging.

Teaching *Heel (Walk Nicely on Leash)*

1. Start with your Boston sitting at your left side. Allow the leash to run loosely through your left hand, with the excess looped in your right.
2. Say "Heel!" and step out on your left foot.
3. When he moves forward, praise "Yes!" and give the treat.
4. If he lags behind, encourage him by patting your leg and calling his name.
5. If he pulls, turn and walk in the opposite direction. (Do this every time he pulls.)
6. Give plenty of praise when your dog walks at your side on a loose leash.
7. To improve his skills, begin to alternate your pace between fast and slow. Then add some left, right, and about-turns to your pattern.

Never let your Boston off leash near busy roads or in other potentially hazardous situations.

FINDING A PROFESSIONAL TRAINER

Whether you're a new owner or just haven't raised a puppy in a while, a professional trainer can lead group sessions or provide one-on-one instruction in your own home. Some will even board and train your dog for you, returning a well-behaved canine a few weeks later. Of course, the fun of ownership is the bond that develops during training, so you'll want to fully participate in all aspects of your Boston's education—from puppy kindergarten through the more advanced skills required in formal obedience.

To locate a qualified trainer, ask your breeder, veterinarian, and dog-owning friends and neighbors for their recommendations. The APDT and National Association of Dog Obedience Instructors (NADOI) (www.nadoi.org) provide membership lists on their websites.

With a few names in hand, contact the trainers and make an appointment to ask questions and observe a class in progress. Find out their educational backgrounds, how long they have been involved with training, class sizes, whether they are familiar with Bostons, and whether they use positive training methods. Watch for any biases, such as that the breed is stubborn or difficult to train. Also, check whether they hold any certifications, such as "Certified Professional Dog Trainer–Knowledge Assessed" from the Certification Council for Pet Dog Trainers (CCPDT) (www.ccpdt.org). To gain certification, a trainer must have at least 300 hours of experience, professional references, and pass a comprehensive written exam.

Remember that dog training need not end with the first course but can quickly become a lifelong passion. If you and your Boston Terrier enjoy learning new skills and working together as a team, there is no limit to what you both can achieve.

SOLVING PROBLEMS
WITH YOUR
BOSTON TERRIER

Problem behaviors contribute to the surrender of nearly 2 million dogs of all breeds each year in the United States. Serious actions, such as aggression and biting, are the most common behavior-related reasons why owners no longer can keep their pets at home. However, simple unruliness can also tip the balance, even when other factors, such as housing and income, are primary. Early socialization and basic training are keys to preventing a breakdown in the human–animal bond. In fact, owners who have taught their dogs basic manners—and maintain realistic expectations of canine conduct—rarely give up their pets. Problem behaviors tend to worsen if not promptly addressed, but with consistency and patience—along with professional intervention, if needed—it's possible to train a dog even when his poor habits are firmly entrenched.

Basic training is key to preventing problem behaviors in your Boston.

WHAT IS A PROBLEM BEHAVIOR?

Just as Boston Terriers vary in temperament, from mellow to excitable, they also differ in their basic personalities. Some learn the ropes quickly, rarely setting a paw out of place. Others seem to thrive on constantly testing their limits. Why is the puppy who aced obedience class now a little terror at home? Surprisingly, some of the same qualities that endear the breed to those who love them also lead to misbehavior when not properly channeled into positive outlets. For example, sociable dogs tend to bark excessively when isolated from household activities or enthusiastically jump up to greet visitors. Those who become easily bored without mental stimulation may take up chewing and digging as interesting pastimes. As we examine the most common problems—barking, chewing, digging, house soiling, jumping up, and nipping—don't lose hope. Bostons want nothing more than to please their owners. With consistency and patience, along with a positive attitude, you'll soon agree with the breed's legion of fanciers who call the Boston Terrier the "best dog in the world."

NOTHING IN LIFE IS FREE (NILF)

When a group of owners was polled for workable solutions to problem behaviors, many suggested a system called "Nothing in Life Is Free" (NILF). This positive training method is based on the premise that owners maintain their leadership roles within the human–canine pack by controlling access to sought-after resources. Dogs must earn attention and walks, food and treats, and toys and playtime by performing simple tasks requested by their owners. For example, a dog must sit on command before he gets his dinner bowl. When he obeys, he receives his reward. Until he complies, no dinner. Bostons catch on very quickly to this method of training, which prohibits any type of correction or discipline. NILF not only benefits pushy dogs but also aids submissive pets who crave security. Both become more confident and relaxed as their roles within the pack are defined under trustworthy human leadership.

HOW TO PRACTICE NILF

1. Teach your Boston a few tasks or tricks that he will be asked to perform on command. Be sure that he fully understands what is expected of him before you begin NILF training.

With their agreeable temperaments, Bostons want nothing more than to please their owners.

2. Before you hand him a favorite toy or treat, give the command. Use an upbeat tone of voice, and make achievement fun for your dog. If he obeys, hand him the toy or treat. If he ignores your command, walk away and try again a few minutes later.

3. Be consistent—don't give in until he performs the task or trick.

4. Be patient as your Boston learns that you now control his access to resources—Nothing in Life Is Free!

COMMON PROBLEM BEHAVIORS

The following are some common problem behaviors that may affect your Boston, as well as techniques to help manage them.

BARKING

Bostons generally are not a barky breed.

They emit low-pitched growly woofs when strangers approach their territory and yip with excitement during playtime. This is a natural behavior for dogs—it's their way to communicate vital information about sights, smells, and sounds to their human and canine buddies. Most Bostons avoid constant yapping and sound the alarm only when they have legitimate concerns. The degree of barking varies among individuals even within the same household. Some rarely bark until a noisier member arrives, who then encourages the others to join in. In multi-dog families, most owners can tell their Bostons apart based on their vocalizations. For example, one dog's unique play-bark sounds like "Hubba! Hubba!" His owner said it's a big hit at the dog park, where someone even recorded it to use as his cell phone ringtone!

How to Manage It

The goal isn't to eliminate barking altogether but to check unwanted outbursts. Teach your Boston the *quiet* command and/or have him go to his bed or crate to calm down.

1. Allow two or three warning barks, then praise with "Good dog!"
2. Say "Quiet!" and the moment he stops barking, give a treat. Never shout commands, or he'll think you're joining him in the commotion.
3. Say "Go to your place!" to have him get in his bed or crate. Offer a chew toy or treat as soon as he settles down. Make his special place fun—not a place of punishment.

Barking is a natural behavior for dogs, although Boston Terriers are generally not a barky breed.

4. If specific noises provoke barking, try a desensitization CD. Introduce the sounds at low volume and gradually increase it over the course of days or weeks to prevent a reaction. Lower the volume if at any point barking ensues.
5. Praise your Boston whenever he's behaving quietly.
6. Be consistent and patient. Make certain that all family members enforce the rules.

   Never resort to harsh scolding or physical discipline to correct barking (or any problem behavior).

CHEWING

His fleece dog bed lies in tatters, stuffing scattered like an indoor snowfall. The homework you left out now resembles bits of confetti. Dogs chew. It usually begins in puppyhood, between three and nine months of age, when Bostons go through the uncomfortable teething stage. Chewing not only helps to relieve the pain associated with emerging adult teeth but is also how puppies learn about the interesting new objects that make up their world. The behavior can persist into adulthood, when dogs become bored and seek attention, or when they experience anxiety from being left alone for long periods. Chewing also stems from a lack of mental stimulation and physical exercise. The adage "a tired dog is a good dog" especially holds true with this bright and energetic breed.

BE AWARE!

Reward good behavior instead of reinforcing negative actions. For example, don't pick up a barking dog and cuddle him, or he'll learn to bark whenever he wants attention.

How to Manage It

To curb chewing, use a crate or an ex-pen to confine your Boston whenever you're unable to closely supervise his actions.

1. To curb destructive chewing, begin by carefully puppy-proofing your home. Remove all temptations within reach, such as children's gear, newspapers, and shoes and socks. Keep electric cords out of reach or wrap exposed cords with pet-safe, repellant-infused cord protectors.

2. Use a crate, ex-pen, or gates to confine your Boston whenever you're unable to closely supervise his actions.

3. Offer an assortment of safe toys, such as dental chews and hard rubber toys stuffed with treats. Avoid squeaky toys or rawhides, which can be harmful—even deadly—if small pieces break off and are then swallowed. Visit the "Boston Terrier Challenge Dog Toy Test" (www.boston-terrier-challenge.com) for reviews of Boston-approved toys.

SOLVING PROBLEMS WITH YOUR BOSTON TERRIER

109

4. If you catch him gnawing an unacceptable object, tell him "No!" and substitute a chew toy. Spray a bitter-tasting repellant on forbidden items, and install anti-chew strips on hard surfaces like baseboards.

5. Praise enthusiastically whenever you find him chewing an appropriate toy.

6. To relieve the discomfort of teething, give your puppy a chilled teether from the freezer or apply an over-the-counter teething gel to sore gums.

7. Adults who chew from boredom or frustration need interactive toys, such as those that challenge them to find treats hidden inside compartments.

8. Remember that Bostons want nothing more than to participate in family fun. Don't isolate your Boston for long periods—look for activities you both can share.

Bostons have preferences about their outdoor duties—they don't enjoy getting chilled!

Never give your Boston old shoes to chew unless you want him to add his tooth marks to your new footwear as well.

DIGGING

Although the breed's terrier roots would suggest otherwise, most Bostons are not aggressive diggers. Some bury favorite bones, whereas others excavate cool places in which to sleep. Bostons have been known to raid the backyard garden as well to savor a hearty mix of vegetables. The key to preventing destructive digging is to monitor your dog whenever he's outdoors and not leave him to his own devices when it comes to landscaping.

How to Manage It

1. Bostons can't tolerate extremes of heat and cold, so most of their outdoor activity should be limited to supervised play in a fenced-in yard.

2. If your Boston enjoys digging, create a special area or install a sandbox where he can burrow to his heart's content.

3. Hide a few toys or treats for him to unearth.
4. If you catch him digging someplace off-limits, say "No!" and take him to the proper spot. Consider fencing off prized flower and vegetable beds to prevent destruction (and consumption).
5. Praise enthusiastically when he digs in his own area.

Never give unrestricted access to the backyard, such as through an open doggy door, when you're unable to closely supervise your Boston's actions.

HOUSE SOILING

Is it too hot or too cold, raining or snowing? Bostons have definite preferences about their outdoor duties—and it doesn't include getting heated or chilled, or the indignity of wet feet! Unfortunately, during inclement weather you may find an unwanted puddle or pile in the unlikeliest of places. Yet because house soiling is a complex problem—with behavioral as well as physical bases—it's important to correctly pinpoint the specific factors involved. For example, does your Boston have a urinary tract infection that increases his urgency? Has a recent food change led to diarrhea? Is he drinking more water than usual? Ask your veterinarian to run a blood panel to rule out infections, hormonal disorders, and heart, kidney, and liver abnormalities.

If your Boston is otherwise healthy, investigate possible behavioral causes. Excitement urination and submissive urination are common among puppies. The former happens during greetings and playtime, whereas the latter results when timid youngsters experience loud noises, scolding, or other frightening events. Separation anxiety, due to the stress of being left alone, and incomplete housetraining also cause soiling.

Never punish your dog for house soiling, especially after the fact! It won't help and will likely make the problem worse. Just clean up the mess and remove all traces of odor with an enzymatic cleaner. Use a black (ultraviolet) light that reveals hard-to-find stains from feces, urine, and vomit. Any odors left behind will trigger repeat incidents in the same spot. Keep in mind that your Boston isn't misbehaving out of spite. By carefully observing his body language—and teaching him a special cue to let you know that he needs to go out—you can prevent all but the most urgent episodes of house soiling. And a

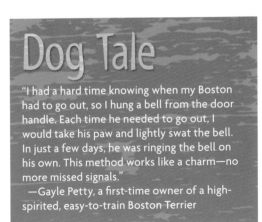

Dog Tale

"I had a hard time knowing when my Boston had to go out, so I hung a bell from the door handle. Each time he needed to go out, I would take his paw and lightly swat the bell. In just a few days, he was ringing the bell on his own. This method works like a charm—no more missed signals."
—Gayle Petty, a first-time owner of a high-spirited, easy-to-train Boston Terrier

rain jacket and warm sweater would be much appreciated!

Age-Related Incontinence: Characterized by dribbling or the loss of urine during sleep, incontinence affects up to 2 million elderly female dogs annually in the United States. Although incontinence can occur in young dogs, as well as in males, spayed females are at the greatest risk due to their reduced levels of estrogen. To properly regulate urination, the bladder's sphincter muscle—controlled by the nervous system—remains closed until a dog needs to urinate. Estrogen is a key hormone in providing tone to the sphincter. When the muscle relaxes too much, she involuntarily leaks urine.

One treatment method is to supplement this lack of estrogen with replacement hormones. Short-acting natural estrogens are preferred over the older synthetic hormones. However, the medication of choice is phenylpropanolamine (PPA), a non-hormonal drug that acts directly on the sympathetic nervous system. By stimulating receptors in the urethra, PPA increases the sphincter's tone to alleviate urine leakage. Improvement may be seen in as little as a week. Side effects are rare but include loss of appetite, restlessness, and increased blood pressure. PPA may be combined with estrogen, if needed, and must be continued for the lifetime of the pet.

Clean stains and remove housetraining accident odors with an enzymatic cleaner.

Urine Marking: More likely among intact than neutered males, urine marking isn't a house-soiling issue but rather a territorial behavior. It's how dogs—even some dominant females—claim particular objects or areas as their own. Any vertical surface, along with new purchases and items belonging to visitors, is at risk. Marking often takes place outdoors as a signal to neighborhood dogs but is highly unacceptable when it happens indoors. Neutering as early as your veterinarian recommends usually reduces or prevents marking altogether. If the behavior has become a habit, however, additional training may be needed. Watch your Boston closely for signs that he's about to lift his leg. Say "No!" and take him outside to urinate. Praise enthusiastically when he performs correctly. Some owners have broken this practice by having their males temporarily wear no-leak wraps (belly bands) that serve as an unpleasant reminder to stay dry. (Change the band if it becomes wet.) When you're unable to supervise, confine your Boston to his crate.

How to Manage It

1. Have your veterinarian rule out infections, hormonal disorders, and other illnesses that may cause house soiling.
2. When these factors have been eliminated, return to the basic steps in

housetraining. Feed and water at the same times each day, and follow a regular schedule of walks. Also, take your dog outside as soon as he wakes up in the morning, after meals, following naps and play sessions, and just before bedtime.

3. Remember that puppies and seniors may need to go out more often than do healthy adults.

4. For excitement urination, greet your puppy in a low-key manner and move vigorous playtime outdoors. Avoid petting or praising after urination, which may inadvertently reinforce this behavior.

5. For submissive urination, kneel down instead of hovering over your dog, don't stare directly into his eyes, and pet under his chin rather than on top of his head. Build his confidence with positive training and socialization experiences.

6. For age-related incontinence, ask your veterinarian whether phenylpropanolamine (PPA) and/or estrogen would be beneficial. Take your senior outside more often, put down piddle pads, and use washable, waterproof bedding.

7. For urine marking, have your Boston neutered as early as your veterinarian recommends. Try no-leak wraps indoors. Clean stains and remove odor with an enzymatic cleaner.

Never resort to scolding or physical discipline to correct house-soiling accidents. Instilling anxiety and fear only makes the problem more difficult to correct.

JUMPING UP

According to those who know and love them, Bostons are hardwired to jump up on people. It stems from their innate excitement in greeting family members and newcomers alike. Dogs also jump up to seek attention, which may be accompanied by another endemic trait—licking! Bostons tend to lick nearly everything in sight, from other living creatures to inanimate objects.

One of the main roadblocks to enforcing proper habits is ambivalence on the part of owners. Some actively encourage their Bostons to jump up and appreciate rambunctious (and wet) welcomes. However, not everyone feels the same way—especially when it comes to muddy paws on clean clothing or sharp toenails scraping bare legs. Good manners are essential in public because your Boston serves as an ambassador of his breed during interactions with small children, the elderly, and others who may be uncomfortable around animals.

How to Manage It

The keys to correcting jumping up are to start as soon as you bring your new puppy home—before bad habits have become firmly established—and to be sure that all family members are on board with the program.

1. When your Boston starts to jump up to gain your attention, turn away to the side and ignore him. Don't touch, speak to, or make eye contact with him. Wait out his peskiness.
2. As soon as he puts all four feet on the ground, praise and give a small treat. Now he has earned your attention. This reinforces that calm—not wild—behavior gains a reward.
3. When visitors arrive, place him in a *sit-stay* or *down-stay*. Or teach him to go to his crate to enjoy a chew toy. Enlist the help of a friend, if needed, to practice these polite greetings.
4. Be consistent and patient as you and your Boston work on breaking this deeply ingrained behavior.

Never use your foot or knee—or *any* physical contact—to correct unwanted jumping.

NIPPING

No one appreciates a puppy who sinks his needle-sharp teeth into flesh. Puppies use their mouths much as we do our hands—to grab and explore objects that catch their fancy—and they typically nip as part of greeting rituals and playful interactions. Most quickly learn by tussling with their littermates that some bites can hurt. The injured party usually yelps in pain and stops playing with the nipper, sending the clear message that the game has become too rough. Puppies who leave the nest too early, before 8 to 12 weeks of age, may not have mastered bite inhibition—the ability to control the force of their jaws. It's up to their owners to continue this vital aspect of training.

To prevent nipping—and possibly future biting—only tolerate polite play.

How to Manage It

1. Require polite play from the start—don't tolerate nipping just because you have a cute puppy. This behavior won't be welcome later when your Boston develops strong teeth and powerful jaws.
2. When he nips, say "Ouch!" and immediately stop all interactions until he calms down.
3. When he plays nicely, praise enthusiastically

Boston Terrier puppies need plenty of physical exercise and mental stimulation to prevent nuisance behaviors, such as barking, chewing, and digging.

and offer a treat.

4. Avoid games like tug-of-war and wrestling, which may encourage nipping.

5. Be sure that all household members enforce "no-nipping" rules.

6. If this behavior escalates to aggression or biting, see the section "Finding Professional Help," below.

Never force your Boston's muzzle closed to teach a no-nipping lesson.

FINDING PROFESSIONAL HELP

Potentially dangerous problems, such as aggression and biting, stem from a variety of environmental, hereditary, and physical factors and require prompt intervention before they become too deeply rooted to correct. Be sure to have your veterinarian rule out any underlying medical disorders that are known to affect behavior: bacterial and viral infections, brain tumors, epilepsy, head injuries, hypothyroidism, and low blood sugar. Genetics also plays a role—two genes, to date, have been linked to aggression in dogs. Providing solutions for major problem behaviors is beyond the scope of this book. Therefore, the services of a knowledgeable specialist are mandatory. In fact, any annoyance that persists—barking, chewing, digging, house soiling, jumping up, or nipping—benefits from the supervised instruction of an experienced professional.

To locate a qualified behaviorist, ask for recommendations from your veterinarian, breeder, or local kennel club. The field of behavioral medicine is one of the newest veterinary specialties. Until the 1980s, most problems fell to dog trainers who may or may not have had the expertise to properly assist owners and their pets. The American College of Veterinary Behaviorists (ACVB) (www.dacvb.org) certifies veterinarians who have completed two-year residencies and passed exams in animal behavior. The American Veterinary Society of Animal Behavior (AVSAB) (www.avsabonline.org) comprises veterinarians and other individuals who hold doctorates in animal behavior. Both websites, which include membership lists, feature informative articles on a number of canine behavior topics. For certified trainers who use positive methods, contact the Association of Pet Dog Trainers (APDT) (www.apdt.com).

SOLVING PROBLEMS WITH YOUR BOSTON TERRIER

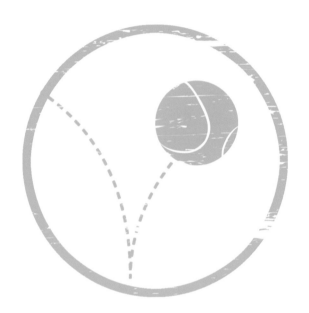

ACTIVITIES WITH YOUR BOSTON TERRIER

If you're looking for some new pastimes—in addition to walks in the neighborhood and trips to the dog park—why not share one or more of these fun activities with your canine best friend? Sharp and quick, Boston Terriers are eager to learn—the more challenging the task, the better. Organized events, whether competitive or cooperative, enhance the bond you have together as each learns a different set of skills. So check out the activities listed below and get started today!

The versatile Boston Terrier can participate in a wide range of activities.

SPORTS AND ACTIVITIES

What special talents does your Boston possess? If he is athletic and loves to run and jump, consider the fast-paced sports of agility and flyball. If he thrives on following instructions and precise execution, perhaps formal obedience is his specialty. Or if sitting quietly in someone's lap and giving gentle doggy kisses is more his style, he may volunteer his services as a therapy dog. Attend training classes and performance events as a spectator to gauge which activities you and your Boston might like to try.

AKC S.T.A.R. PUPPY® PROGRAM

Every puppy is a star in his own household, but is your Boston a S.T.A.R. Puppy? S.T.A.R., which stands for *socialization, training, activity*, and *responsibility*, is the American Kennel Club's (AKC) most recent program to reward basic training and responsible pet ownership. Any puppy who completes at least six weeks of training in a class taught by an AKC-approved instructor qualifies for the S.T.A.R. Puppy test.

Consisting of three parts—owner, puppy, and pre-Canine Good Citizen (CGC) behaviors—the test includes the Responsible Dog Owner's Pledge (see below) and puppy skills such as coming when called, walking a brief distance on a leash, and performing the *down, sit,* and *stay* commands. Upon passing the test, you'll receive an application for enrollment in the S.T.A.R. Puppy Program, which, for a small fee, includes a certificate and canine medal, the *AKC Puppy Handbook*, and other benefits. To locate a trainer in your area, log on to the AKC's website (www. akc.org) and enter your state in the drop-down box.

AKC CANINE GOOD CITIZEN® PROGRAM

Developed in 1989 by the AKC, the CGC Program encourages responsible pet care for owners and basic manners for dogs. This two-part test consists of the Responsible Dog Owner's Pledge, in which you agree to provide for your Boston's health needs (veterinary care, adequate food and water, daily exercise, and regular grooming), ensure his safety (proper identification, adhering to leash laws, and using fencing when appropriate), prevent nuisance behavior (curb excessive barking and pick up and dispose of waste), and attend to his overall quality of life (playtime and basic training).

Wearing a buckle or slip collar and on leash, your dog must pass the following steps:

The Canine Good Citizen (CGC) Program encourages responsible pet care for owners and basic manners for dogs.

1. Allow the evaluator to approach him and talk to you.
2. Sit politely as the evaluator pets him on his head and body.
3. Permit gentle brushing and examination of his ears and paws and be in clean and healthy condition.
4. Walk nicely on a loose leash, making left, right, and about-turns with signals to stop in between turns and at the finish.
5. Walk nicely among a group of strangers.
6. Respond to the *down*, *sit*, and *stay* commands.
7. Come when called.
8. Behave appropriately when the evaluator and her dog approach, stop, and shake your hand.
9. React confidently to distractions, such as a dropped object or unexpected noise.
10. Maintain training when left alone with the evaluator while you are out of sight for a short period.

If your Boston passed the test, return the form to the AKC with a small fee to receive your certificate. Also, check out the S.T.A.R. Puppy- and CGC-logo merchandise—tags, medallions, patches, and more—on the AKC's website.

AGILITY

Bostons running in equestrian events! What would Robert C. Hooper, who is not only credited with founding the breed but also brought about a revival in steeplechase, think about canine agility? First seen more than three decades ago at England's Crufts Dog Show, when members of the entertainment committee put on a small-scale demonstration between group judging, agility has become the fastest-growing canine sport on both sides of the Pond. Based on the jumps and barriers of National Hunt Racing, handlers and their dogs run a timed course that consists of jumps (tire, wall, broad, and bar) and obstacles (tunnels, weave poles, seesaw, A-frame, dogwalk, and pause table) taken in a specific order. Dogs perform off leash, responding only to their handlers' verbal commands and physical signals. No touching or assisting is allowed. The jump heights are modified and time limits adjusted so that breeds of all sizes work on a level playing field. And if you think that small dogs have a disadvantage, consider that the breed with the highest number of Master Agility Champion titles is a . . . Papillon!

Agility Scoring

Dogs begin with a perfect score of 100 points and take deductions for exceeding the course time, missing a contact zone, refusing an obstacle, and other errors. To receive his title, your dog must execute three qualifying runs of 85 or more points from at least two different judges.

In agility, handlers and their dogs run through a timed obstacle course.

Agility Classes

Standard: This class comprises jumps, tunnels, and weave poles, along with contact objects, such as the dogwalk, A-frame, seesaw, and pause table. Dogs must place at least one paw on the painted contact zones, located on the up and down sides of the obstacles, and must sit or lie down for at least five seconds on the pause table.

Jumpers With Weaves: A quick-moving course with no contact objects to slow the momentum, this class consists only of jumps, tunnels, chutes, and weave poles. Dogs execute between 13 and 20 elements, depending on the title for which they are competing.

Fifteen and Send Time (FAST): This class involves negotiating 15 point-valued obstacles and the Send Bonus. The mandatory single-bar jumps and weave poles are combined with an assortment of jumps, tunnels, and a table that have been assigned point values. Dogs must also perform the Send Bonus, in which the handler remains at a specified distance and sends her dog to complete the obstacle.

BE AWARE!
Before you begin any active sport, have your veterinarian verify that your Boston is healthy enough to participate. Check your canine athlete regularly for limping, soreness, or swelling, and be careful not to overtrain him.

Agility Titles

The AKC awards both regular and preferred Novice, Open, and Excellent titles in Standard, Jumpers With Weaves, and FAST categories. (Preferred classes use lower jump heights and give more time to complete the course.) Sweet Sociable Samuel, owned by Nancy Ames, was the first Boston to earn an AKC title in agility.

The top-level Master Agility Champion (MACH) award is presented to dogs who earn at least 750 points and 20 double-qualifying scores in Excellent B Standard or Excellent B Jumpers With Weaves classes. The first Boston to earn his MACH title was Brandy's Ace High Kid, owned and trained by Ann Croft. His sire and dam have also set records in performance events, including the first Flyball Master award for Bostons.

CONFORMATION

If you have an attractive Boston who meets the elements outlined in the standard and boasts a flashy "Look at Me!" attitude, you might enjoy showing him off in the conformation ring. The best way to start is by attending a local show, where you can watch experienced handlers and their dogs compete in Breed Classes and the more challenging Group and Best in Show categories. Sponsoring kennel clubs usually have information available on handling classes and match shows that are open to the public. Although "fun matches" don't award points toward a title, they provide an excellent arena for preparing your dog and practicing your handling techniques. Also, consider becoming a member of your local kennel club, as well as the Boston Terrier Club of America (BTCA). From participating in a variety of activities to volunteering your talents behind the scenes, you'll not only

Conformation evaluates a Boston against the breed standard.

have fun with your dog but also build a nice social circle of friends—others who share a passion for the breed.

Conformation Classes

Bostons at least six months old and free of disqualifying faults may enter one of seven classes to vie for their championship titles: Puppy, Twelve-to-Eighteen Month, Novice, Amateur-Owner-Handler, Bred-by-Exhibitor, American-Bred, or Open. Each class is divided into sections for dogs (males) and bitches (females). Because your Boston may qualify for more than one class—Puppy and Novice, for example—always select the category in which he stands the best chance of finishing undefeated. (The seven class winners are the only dogs who go on to compete for points at a given show.)

Earning Points

If your Boston won a blue ribbon in his class, he will return for the Winners Class. First, all the prize-winning males from each of the classes compete for Winners Dog—the only male who receives points toward his championship. The second-place finisher earns the title Reserve Winners. Next, the female class winners vie for Winners Bitch—the female who receives points—and Reserve Winners. Finally, the Winners Dog and Winners Bitch join champions of record and dogs who have

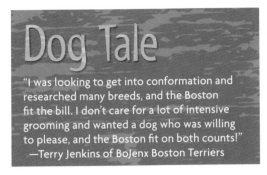
completed the requirements for their championships to compete for Best of Breed. If your Boston wins Best of Breed at an all-breed show, he *may* go on to the Non-Sporting Group, and if he wins first place, he then *must* compete with the other six winners for Best in Show.

Champion of Record: When a dog accumulates 15 points, he becomes a champion of record and is entitled to place the prefix "Ch." before his registered name. He must win six or more points at two shows—three or more points (called a "major") at each show—from two different judges. An additional judge (or judges) awards the remaining points. The number of points a dog can win ranges from zero to five, depending on how many dogs he defeats that day. If the Winners Dog or Winners Bitch wins Best of Breed, for instance, all Best of Breed competitors are counted to determine the points. If a dog wins the Non-Sporting Group or Best in Show, he takes the highest number of points (usually five) earned in Group or Best in Show judging. An excellent Boston, therefore, can become a champion in three shows by winning three 5-point majors.

Grand Champion: The AKC instituted the Grand Champion title in 2009 for champions who earn a total of 25 points, including at least three major wins under four judges. The dog also must have defeated at least one champion at three shows. Two years later, the AKC added Achievement Levels—Bronze, Silver, Gold, and Platinum—for dogs who accumulate 100, 200, 400, and 800 points, respectively. In 2010, GCH Ken's N' Roobarb N' The Horse Ya Rode In On, bred by Barbara Rooney and owned by Ken Roux and Vicky Wilt, became the breed's first Grand Champion. Known as Hoss, he also won Best of Breed at the 2011 Westminster Kennel Club Dog Show and ranked as the number-one Boston Terrier in the United States.

Junior Showmanship

Young members of the fancy who participate in Junior Showmanship have the opportunity to learn the correct method of handling their chosen breeds, hone their skills, gain experience before entering regular classes, and develop good sportsmanship—win or lose. Categories include Junior and Senior divisions, based on handlers' ages, and Novice and Open sections, according to the number of first-place prizes won. Unlike standard show competition, Juniors are judged solely on their handling skills. The merits of their dogs are not a factor. Bostons are a popular choice because of their easy-to-handle size, simple grooming requirements, and willingness to do what is asked of them.

FLYBALL

This fast-paced sport originated four decades ago, when a group of trainers in southern California threw tennis balls to their dogs at the end of a hurdle-racing event. It gained national attention in the late 1970s, after the inventor of the first ball-launching box, Herbert Wagner, gave a demonstration on *The Tonight Show Starring Johnny Carson*. The first flyball tournament took place in 1983, and the next year a dozen teams from the Toronto–Detroit area formed the North American Flyball Association (NAFA). Today, more than 16,000 dogs and 700 dog training clubs compete under NAFA guidelines.

Flyball is a relay-style race in which two 4-dog teams run side by side against one another. Each dog runs the length of the 51-foot (15.5-m) track, jumping hurdles spaced 10 feet (3 m) apart. The height of the hurdles is 4 inches (10 cm) less than the shortest dog's height at the withers, so including a small dog lowers the jump height for the entire team. At the end of the track, the dog steps on a spring-loaded box that releases a tennis ball. He grabs the ball in his mouth as quickly as possible and returns across the hurdles to the starting line. Only when the previous dog crosses the line does the next dog take his turn. The first team that finishes without errors wins the heat and progresses to the next round. The top flyball team in the United States holds the NAFA World Record at 15.22 seconds!

Flyball Scoring

Each member of the winning team receives points based on the time it takes all four members to accurately complete the course. Teams that finish in less than 32 seconds give each dog 1 point; 28 seconds, 5 points; and 24 seconds, 25 points. Races use electronic judging systems equipped with lights and infrared timing sensors to record starts, finishes, and times to one-thousandth of a second.

Flyball Titles

NAFA awards titles based on the number of points a dog accumulates in his lifetime. Those who earn 20 points receive the title Flyball Dog (FD), followed by Flyball Dog Excellent (FDX) and Flyball Dog Champion (FDCH). At 5,000 points, dogs earn Flyball Master (FM), followed by Flyball Master Excellent (FMX) and

Obedience exercises are evaluated on a point scale, based on the judge's mental picture of the ideal performance.

Flyball Master Champion (FMCH). At 20,000 points, they earn the ONYX title, followed by Flyball Grand Champion (FGDCH), and—for dogs with at least 100,000 points—the prestigious Hobbes Award. Ch. Brandy's Doc Holliday, owned by Bruce and Sandy Crook, was the first Boston to earn the FDCH and FM titles; Eli, owned by Gary and Sue Herber, the first FMX; and Tumbelina, owned by Jenny Graziano, the first FMCH, ONYX, and FGDCH. Anita LaPlante's Megabyte stands atop the breed's leaderboard with more than 53,500 points!

OBEDIENCE

If you and your Boston enjoyed the special bond the two of you developed in working toward the CGC title, consider delving into the more challenging arena of competitive obedience. Conceived by Helene Whitehouse Walker, who sought to demonstrate the trainability of her Standard Poodles, the nation's first all-breed obedience test took place in 1933 on her estate in Mount Kisco, New York. Today, the AKC sponsors more than 2,500 obedience trials, with nearly 100,000 dogs participating annually. Dogs compete at three levels—Novice, Open, and Utility—which are available to purebred and mixed breeds alike. If you own an unregistered dog, such as an adopted or rescued pet, request a Purebred Alternative Listing/Indefinite Listing Privilege (PAL/ILP) number from the AKC so that your dog can participate in all obedience and performance events.

Obedience Scoring

Exercises are evaluated on a point scale based on the judge's mental picture of the ideal performance. "Willingness, enjoyment, and precision" on the part of the dog and "naturalness, gentleness, and smoothness" in handling are key elements of the AKC's regulations. Each dog starts with a perfect score of 200 and then loses points for mistakes like sitting crookedly, failing to come when called, or retrieving the wrong object. Handling errors, such as giving multiple commands or using physical assistance, result in deductions as well. To earn a qualifying score, called a "leg," toward a title, your Boston must achieve half of the required points in each exercise for a minimum of 170 points. After three qualifying scores from three different judges, your dog will receive his title.

Obedience Classes

Novice: The beginning level, which grants the title Companion Dog (CD), consists of the basic commands that all dogs need to know to be good household companions. Exercises include on- and off-leash heeling, standing in place for inspection by the judge, coming when called, and sitting and lying down for a pre-set length of time.

   Open: The next level, which grants the title Companion Dog Excellent (CDX), is more difficult than Novice. Exercises include heeling off leash in different patterns, dropping to the *down* position during the *recall*, retrieving a dumbbell on the flat jump as well as over the high jump, leaping the broad jump, and sitting and lying down while the owner waits outside the ring.

Utility: The highest level, which challenges even the brightest Bostons—along with their handlers—grants the title Utility Dog (UD). Exercises include off-leash heeling with hand signals to stand, stay, drop, sit, and come, locating two articles by scent, standing for examination, and directed retrieving and jumping.

Special Awards: After your dog has earned his CDX and UD titles, he may continue to compete for the Utility Dog Excellent (UDX) award. Your Boston must earn qualifying scores in both Open B and Utility B at ten additional trials. Those who have earned their UD titles also receive points when they place first or second in Open B or Utility B competition. To qualify as Obedience Trial Champion (OTCH), your dog must have won three first prizes (one each in Open and Utility) from three different judges. He must also have accumulated 100 points based on the number of dogs he defeated. The letters "OTCH," unlike most obedience designations, precede the official registered name. The first Boston to earn his OTCH was Brother Mack Duff, owned by Ellen Dresselhuis.

Versatile Companion Dog

Bostons who earn titles in agility, obedience, *and* tracking qualify for the title Versatile Companion Dog (VCD) in four progressive levels that reflect the difficulty of their feats. In 2005, Skyfall's Sweet Sonic Boom, owned by Nancy Ames, attained VCD1, and the following year, Janet V. Rey's Ch. Chelestina's Star Romancer earned VCD2. The most advanced Versatile Companion Champion (VCCH) award goes to those who have completed the titles Obedience Trial Champion (OTCH), Master Agility Champion (MACH), and Champion Tracker (CT).

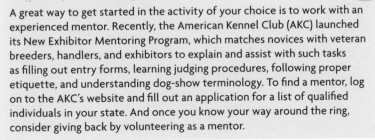

PUPPY POINTER

A great way to get started in the activity of your choice is to work with an experienced mentor. Recently, the American Kennel Club (AKC) launched its New Exhibitor Mentoring Program, which matches novices with veteran breeders, handlers, and exhibitors to explain and assist with such tasks as filling out entry forms, learning judging procedures, following proper etiquette, and understanding dog-show terminology. To find a mentor, log on to the AKC's website and fill out an application for a list of qualified individuals in your state. And once you know your way around the ring, consider giving back by volunteering as a mentor.

RALLY

Similar to rally-style auto racing, in which drivers proceed at their own pace following a written set of directions to reach their destination, this AKC event began in 2005 as a bridge between the CGC program and formal obedience and agility. A judge sets up a unique course at each trial and posts a map at ringside. You may walk the course ahead of time—without your Boston—to become familiar with the exercises. When the judge gives the "Forward!" command, you and your dog execute a series of marked stations that feature both stationary and moving skills, turns in different directions, changes of pace, and walking around pylons in specific patterns. In rally, unlike formal obedience, you may give your dog multiple commands, encouragement, and praise. Any command that is deemed too harsh is penalized, and touching or physical corrections are not allowed.

To qualify as a therapy dog, your Boston must be sociable, gentle, calm, and well behaved.

Rally Scoring

Dogs begin with a perfect score of 100 and lose points for poor *sits*, touching a pylon, knocking over a jump, or not performing the skill. Handling errors, such as using a tight leash, giving a loud command, or poor teamwork, also result in deductions. Although teams are timed, course times are only used as tiebreakers if more than one team receives the same number of points. After three qualifying scores of 70 or better from at least two different judges, your dog will earn his title.

Rally Classes

Novice: The beginning level, which grants the title Rally Novice (RN), consists of 10 to 15 stations, with 3 to 5 stationary skills, like *sit* or *down,* that show your dog's knowledge of basic commands. The entire course is performed on leash, and perfect *heel* position is not required.

   Advanced: The next level, Rally Advanced (RA), is progressively more difficult. The course includes 12 to 17 stations, 3 to 7 stationary exercises, 3 advanced skills, and a jump (broad, high, or bar jump). This course is performed off leash.

Excellent: The highest level, Rally Excellent (RE), requires 15 to 20 stations, 3 to 7 stationary exercises, 3 advanced- and 2 excellent-level skills, and 2 jumps. It also includes an Honor Exercise, in which your dog must remain in an assigned *sit* or *down* position—without moving—while a second *running* dog completes his turn at the course.

Special Awards: The title Rally Advanced Excellent (RAE) is awarded to dogs who qualify in both Rally Advanced B and Rally Excellent B at ten separate trials.

THERAPY

As the most popular breed from the 1920s through the 1940s, this distinctive black-and-white dog easily rekindles many seniors' memories of their childhood "Boston bulls," as they were once known. Their cheerful dispositions combined with their playful demeanors make them excellent canine ambassadors for those confined to hospitals, nursing and rehabilitation facilities, and others simply in need of friendly visitors.

To qualify as a therapy dog, your Boston must be sociable, gentle, calm, and well behaved—even when confronted with distractions and unfamiliar sights and sounds. He must enjoy being petted and stroked and be content to sit in the laps of strangers. If he doesn't mind dressing up in costumes, knows a few tricks, or has a unique "shtick," so much the better.

To get started, you'll need to decide whether to visit facilities solo or as part of an organized group. Contact the administrator or activity director in advance for permission to bring your Boston on a convenient date and time. Always be prompt and reliable, as many residents set their schedules around the daily event calendar. Several organizations screen and test dogs for their suitability for therapy work, including the Delta Society (www.deltasociety.org), Therapy Dogs Inc. (www.therapydogs.com), and Therapy Dogs International (TDI) (www.tdi-dog.org).

TRAVELING WITH YOUR BOSTON

The Boston's lively and inquisitive nature, coupled with his portable size, makes him an ideal travel companion. Yet whether your plans include a weekend getaway or the Grand Tour, you'll need to prepare early if you want your four-legged friend to join you on your journey. Schedule an appointment with your veterinarian to make certain that all inoculations—especially rabies—are current and your pet is fit to travel. Most destinations require a health certificate signed by a veterinarian within ten days of departure. Even if you travel within the United States, a health certificate will enable you to board your dog for the day at major tourist attractions. If you plan to travel abroad, find out the entry regulations for pets. For example, to visit a European Union (EU) member nation without a lengthy quarantine, dogs must carry Pet Passports that contain specific records required under the Pet Travel Scheme. Websites, including www.dogfriendly.com and www. pettravel.com, offer a wealth of information for on-the-go owners and their pets. Although traveling with your Boston is more complicated than touring solo, you'll find it a rewarding experience—with memories to last a lifetime. *Bon voyage!*

The Boston's lively and inquisitive nature, coupled with his portable size, makes him an ideal travel companion.

TRAVEL BY CAR

Most Bostons love to go for car rides and have learned to pick up their owners' subtle signals of an impending excursion. They greet the jingling of keys, for instance, with wiggling hindquarters and excited barks that say "Don't forget me!" Start at an early age with short jaunts and fun experiences, and reward good behavior with a favorite treat. Avoid feeding just before an outing to prevent carsickness, but bring along a supply of food and water on extended journeys. Make certain to stop every two to three hours for your Boston to stretch, walk around, and relieve himself, and always clean up afterward. To ensure his safety in a moving vehicle, have him ride in an airline-style carrier secured in place with a seatbelt. Don't let him ride with his head out the window, and wait until his leash is firmly attached to open the car door. It takes only a moment for a dog to escape in an unfamiliar location! Of course, *never* leave your dog in a parked car—Bostons overheat quickly even in the shade, and a closed car can quickly reach oven-like temperatures that may lead to heatstroke or death.

TRAVEL BY AIR

Although airlines successfully transport nearly a half-million animals each year—including top show dogs—the potential risks of shipping by air concern all owners. Fortunately, the Boston's portable size enables him to travel in the passenger cabin as long as he fits into an under-seat crate or other airline-approved carrier. Because only one animal is permitted in each section of the plane, reserve your seat as early as possible. Try to book a direct flight, and avoid weekend or holiday travel, if possible. If you must ship your Boston as cargo, contact the airline well in advance of your departure to verify current regulations. Some airlines ship brachycephalic (short-nosed) breeds only within certain air-temperature ranges, whereas others prohibit them altogether. The Animal Welfare Act, which regulates shipments of animals by air, may be downloaded from the Animal and Plant Health Inspection Service (APHIS) section of the U.S. Department of Agriculture's (USDA) website (www.aphis.usda.gov).

PET-FRIENDLY LODGING

To locate hotels and motels that welcome pets, obtain a copy of *Traveling With Your Pet—The AAA PetBook*, which lists more than 13,000 AAA-rated lodgings and tourist attractions. Also, check out the numerous cell phone apps that direct you to the nearest pet-friendly hotels, groomers, or veterinarians based on your GPS location. Some also store veterinary records, which may be a lifesaver in case of an on-the-road emergency. Always verify the establishment's pet policy in advance, even if you have stayed there before.

To ensure that your Boston Terrier will be a welcome guest wherever he lodges, follow these guidelines:
• Never leave your dog uncrated in your room. Crates not only prevent destructive chewing or accidental escape if a door is left open but could also save your pet's life from room hazards such as insecticides, poisons, cleaning products, or electrical cords.
• Never allow your dog off leash, and make certain that he is wearing an ID tag.
• Always clean up after your pet.
• Never allow him on furniture. If your Boston must sleep in bed with you, bring a blanket from home to place on the sheets.
• Be sure that he doesn't bark when left alone.
• Offer to pay for any damage that your Boston Terrier might accidentally cause.

RESOURCES

ASSOCIATIONS AND ORGANIZATIONS

BREED CLUBS

American Kennel Club (AKC)
8051 Arco Corporate Drive, Suite 100
Raleigh, NC 27617-3390
Telephone: (919) 233-9767
Fax: (919) 233-3627
E-Mail: info@akc.org
www.akc.org

The Boston Terrier Club
www.thebostonterrierclub.co.uk

The Boston Terrier Club of America (BTCA)
www.bostonterrierclubofamerica.org

Boston Terrier Club of Canada (BTCC)
www.bostonterrierclubofcanada.com

Canadian Kennel Club (CKC)
200 Ronson Drive, Suite 400
Etobicoke, Ontario M9W 5Z9
Telephone: (416) 675-5511
Fax: (416) 675-6506
E-Mail: information@ckc.ca
www.ckc.ca

Fédération Cynologique Internationale (FCI)
Secretariat General de la FCI
Place Albert 1er, 13
B – 6530 Thuin
Belgique
www.fci.be

The Kennel Club
1-5 Clarges Street, Piccadilly,
London W1J 8AB
Telephone: 0844 463 3980
Fax: 020 7518 1028
www.the-kennel-club.org.uk

United Kennel Club (UKC)
100 E. Kilgore Road
Kalamazoo, MI 49002-5584
Telephone: (269) 343-9020
Fax: (269) 343-7037
www.ukcdogs.com

GROOMING

How to Dremel Dog Nails
www.doberdawn.com

National Dog Groomers Association of America
P.O. Box 101
Clark, PA 16113
Telephone: (724) 962-2711
Fax: (724) 962-1919
Email: ndga@nationaldoggroomers.com
www.nationaldoggroomers.com

What to Do if Your Boston's Ears Won't Stand Up!
www.boston-terriers.com/ears.htm

PET SITTERS

National Association of Professional Pet Sitters
15000 Commerce Parkway, Suite C
Mt. Laurel, New Jersey 08054
Telephone: (856) 439-0324
Fax: (856) 439-0525
E-Mail: napps@petsitters.org
www.petsitters.org

Pet Sitters International
201 East King Street
King, NC 27021-9161
Telephone: (336) 983-9222
Fax: (336) 983-5266
E-Mail: info@petsit.com
www.petsit.com

RESCUE ORGANIZATIONS AND ANIMAL WELFARE GROUPS

American Humane Association (AHA)
63 Inverness Drive East
Englewood, CO 80112
Telephone: (303) 792-5333
Fax: (303) 792-5333
www.americanhumane.org

American Society for the
Prevention of Cruelty to Animals
(ASPCA)
424 E. 92nd Street
New York, NY 10128-6804
Telephone: (212) 876-7700
www.aspca.org

The Humane Society of the
United States (HSUS)
2100 L Street, NW
Washington DC 20037
Telephone: (202) 452-1100
www.hsus.org

Royal Society for the Prevention
of Cruelty to Animals (RSPCA)
RSPCA Enquiries Service
Wilberforce Way, Southwater,
Horsham, West Sussex RH13 9RS
United Kingdom
www.rspca.org.uk

SPORTS
International Agility Link (IAL)
85 Blackwall Road
Chuwar Qld 4306, Australia
Telephone: 61 (07) 3202 2361
Email: steve@agilityclick.com

North American Dog Agility
Council (NADAC)
P.O. Box 1206
Colbert, OK 74733
Email: info@nadac.com
www.nadac.com

North American Flyball
Association (NAFA)
1333 West Devon Avenue, #512
Chicago, IL 60660
Telephone: (800) 318-6312
Email: flyball@flyball.org
www.flyball.org

United States Dog Agility
Association (USDAA)
P. O. Box 850955
Richardson, TX 75085-0955
Telephone: (972) 487-2200
Fax: (972) 231-9700
www.usdaa.com

THERAPY
Delta Society
875 124th Ave, NE, Suite 101
Bellevue, WA 98005
Telephone: (425) 679-5500
Fax: (425) 679-5539
E-Mail: info@DeltaSociety.org
www.deltasociety.org

Therapy Dogs Inc.
P.O. Box 20227
Cheyenne WY 82003
Telephone: (877) 843-7364
Fax: (307) 638-2079
E-Mail: therapydogsinc@
qwestoffice.net
www.therapydogs.com

Therapy Dogs International (TDI)
88 Bartley Road
Flanders, NJ 07836
Telephone: (973) 252-9800
Fax: (973) 252-7171
E-Mail: tdi@gti.net
www.tdi-dog.org

TRAINING
American College of Veterinary
Behaviorists (ACVB)
Dr. Bonnie V. Beaver, ACVB
Executive Director
College of Veterinary Medicine,
4474 TAMU
Texas A&M University
College Station, Texas 77843-4474
www.dacvb.org

Association of Pet Dog Trainers
(APDT)
101 North Main Street, Suite 610
Greenville, SC 29601
Telephone: (800) PET-DOGS
Fax: (864) 331-0767
E-Mail: information@apdt.com
www.apdt.com

International Association of
Animal Behavior Consultants
(IAABC)
565 Callery Road
Cranberry Township, PA 16066
Telephone: (484) 843-1091
E-Mail: info@iaabc.org
www.iaabc.org

National Association of Dog
Obedience Instructors (NADOI)
P. O. Box 1439
Socorro, NM 87801
Telephone: (505) 850-5957
www.nadoi.org

VETERINARY AND HEALTH RESOURCES

Academy of Veterinary Homeopathy (AVH)
P. O. Box 232282
Leucadia, CA 92023-2282
Telephone: (866) 652-1590
Fax: (866) 652-1590
www.theavh.org

American Academy of Veterinary Acupuncture (AAVA)
P.O. Box 1058
Glastonbury, CT 06033
Telephone: (860) 632-9911
Fax: (860) 659-8772
www.aava.org

American Animal Hospital Association (AAHA)
12575 W. Bayaud Ave.
Lakewood, CO 80228
Telephone: (303) 986-2800
Fax: (303) 986-1700
E-Mail: info@aahanet.org
www.aahanet.org

American College of Veterinary Internal Medicine (ACVIM)
1997 Wadsworth Blvd., Suite A
Lakewood, CO 80214-5293
Telephone: (800) 245-9081
Fax: (303) 231-0880
Email: ACVIM@ACVIM.org
www.acvim.org

American College of Veterinary Ophthalmologists (ACVO)
P.O. Box 1311
Meridian, ID 83860
Telephone: (208) 466-7624
Fax: (208) 466-7693
E-Mail: office11@acvo.com
www.acvo.com

American Heartworm Society (AHS)
P. O. Box 8266
Wilmington, DE 19803-8266
Email: info@heartwormsociety.org
www.heartwormsociety.org

American Holistic Veterinary Medical Association (AHVMA)
P. O. Box 630
Abingdon, MD 21009-0630
Telephone: (410) 569-0795
Fax: (410) 569-2346
E-Mail: office@ahvma.org
www.ahvma.org

American Kennel Club Canine Health Foundation
P. O. Box 900061
Raleigh, NC 27675
Telephone: (888) 682-9696
Fax: (919) 334-4011
www.akcchf.org

American Veterinary Medical Association (AVMA)
1931 North Meacham Road, Suite 100
Schaumburg, IL 60173-4360
Telephone: (800) 248-2862
Fax: (847) 925-1329
E-Mail: avmainfo@avma.org
www.avma.org

Animal Health Trust
DNA Testing for Early-Onset Hereditary Cataracts in Boston Terriers
Lanwades Park, Kentford
Newmarket, Suffolk
CB8 7UU
Telephone: 01638 751000
Fax: 01638 750410
Email: info@aht.org.uk
www.aht.org.uk

ASPCA Animal Poison Control Center
Telephone: (888) 426-4435
www.aspca.org

British Veterinary Association (BVA)
7 Mansfield Street
London
W1G 9NQ
Telephone: 0207 636 6541
Fax: 0207 908 6349
E-Mail: bvahq@bva.co.uk
www.bva.co.uk

Canine Epilepsy Network
www.canine-epilepsy.net

Canine Eye Registration
Foundation (CERF)
VMDB/CERF
1717 Philo Road
Urbana, IL 61803-3007
Telephone: (217) 693-4800
Fax: (217) 693-4801
E-Mail: CERF@vmdb.org
www.vmdb.org

Epilepsy and Seizures in Boston
Terriers
www.boston-terriers.com/
seizures.htm

Glutamate and Aspartate
Restricted Diet
www.dogtorj.com

Orthopedic Foundation for
Animals (OFA)
2300 E. Nifong Boulevard
Columbia, MO 65201-3806
Telephone: (573) 442-0418
Fax: (573) 875-5073
Email: ofa@offa.org
www.offa.org

Rabies Challenge Fund
c/o Hemopet
11561 Salinaz Avenue
Garden Grove, CA 92843
Telephone: (714) 891-2022
Fax: (714) 891-2123
www.rabieschallengefund.org

US Food and Drug Administration
Center for Veterinary Medicine
(CVM)
7519 Standish Place
HFV-12
Rockville, MD 20855-0001
Telephone: (240) 276-9300 or (888)
INFO-FDA
Email: AskCVM@fda.hhs.gov
www.fda.gov/cvm

Veterinary Oral Health Council
(VOHC)
www.vohc.org

Wendy's Dogs Alive Diet—The
Balanced Approach to Safely
Cooking for Your Dog!
www.boston-terriers.com/
dogsalive.htm

PUBLICATIONS

BOOKS

Anderson, Teoti. *The Super Simple Guide to Housetraining*. Neptune City: TFH Publications, Inc., 2004.

Anne, Jonna, with Mary Straus. *The Healthy Dog Cookbook: 50 Nutritious and Delicious Recipes Your Dog Will Love*. UK: Ivy Press Limited, 2008.

Gewirtz, Elaine Waldorf. DogLife *Boston Terrier*. Neptune City: TFH Publications, Inc., 2010.

Libby, Tracy. Terra-Nova *The Boston Terrier*. Neptune City: TFH Publications, Inc., 2005.

MAGAZINES

AKC Family Dog
American Kennel Club
260 Madison Avenue
New York, NY 10016
Telephone: (800) 490-5675
E-Mail: familydog@akc.org
www.akc.org/pubs/familydog

AKC Gazette
American Kennel Club
260 Madison Avenue
New York, NY 10016
Telephone: (800) 533-7323
E-Mail: gazette@akc.org
www.akc.org/pubs/gazette

WEBSITES

Boston Terrier Hub
www.bostonterrierhub.com

Nylabone
www.nylabone.com

TFH Publications, Inc.
www.tfh.com

Woof! A Boston Terrier Board
www.woofboard.com

INDEX

Note: **Boldfaced** pages indicate illustrations.

canned food, 42
carbohydrates in diet, 38
car travel with Bostons, 130
cataracts, hereditary, 81–82
Certification Council for Pet
 Dog Trainers (CCPDT), 103
characteristics of Bostons
    about, 6
    breed-specific health
      problems, 77–84
    breed standard, 8
    deafness and, 79, **80**
    discerning moods of, 22
    environment considerations,
     24
    exercise considerations,
     24–25
    personality, 22–24
    physical, 18–22
    for therapy dogs, **128,** 129
    trainability, 25

typical life spans, 77
Chelestina's Star Romancer
 (dog), 127
cherry eye, 84
chewing behavior, 109–110
children and Bostons, 23, 94
chiropractic therapy, 88
cleft palate, 84
Cleveland, Grover, 8
clipping Bostons nails, 62
clothing (supplies), **29,** 29–30
coat and colors
    breed standard, **19,** 19–21
    grooming considerations,
     53–55
    health considerations, 73–74,
     84–85
collars (supplies), **30,** 30–31, 99
come command, 100
commands. See specific
 commands

commercial food
    about, 41
    canned food, 42
    dry food, 42
    semi-moist food, 43
    therapeutic food, 43
companionability of Bostons,
 23–24
conformation shows, 121–124,
 122
Conroy, John Robert, 12, 14
Cornbill, William, 12
coronavirus, 68–69
Cracksman (dog), 7
crates (supplies), 31–32
crate training, 94–97, **95,** 109
Crook, Bruce and Sandy, 125

D
Dagenais, Lynn, 44
Daley, Mrs. L. B., 12
deafness in Bostons, 79, **80**
Delta Society, 45, 129
dental care, 56–57
diarrhea, 85
digging behavior, 110–111
distemper, 68–69
dog shows, 11–12, 35, 77
down command, 100–101
Dresselhuis, Ellen, 127

E
ear care, 58–60, 79
ear cropping, **60**
ear mites, 73–74
Eli (dog), 125
Emperor's Ace (dog), 12
environment and Bostons, 24
epilepsy, 79–80
essential fatty acids (EFAs), 45
exercise and Bostons, 24–25, 32

ex-pens, 32, 109
eye care, 60–61, 84

F
fat in diet, 39
feeding Bostons
    basic nutrients, 38–41
    commercial food, 41–43
    flatulence and, 85–86
    foods to avoid, 47
    housetraining and, 48, 97
    non-commercial food,
       43–45
    obesity and, 48–49
    probiotics, 46, **46**
    puppy considerations, 40
    scheduling, 48
    supplements, 45–46
    treat considerations, 103
first-aid kits, 88
Fitzgerald, Claude J., 12
flatulence, 85–86
fleas, 72–73
flyball sport, 124–125
food bowls, 32–33, 45
Ford, Gerald R., 15
forward command, 128
Fox, Emma G., 12
free-feeding method, 48

G
gates (supplies), 33, 109
Giardia, 68
glial tumors, 84
Goode's Buster (dog), 7
Graziano, Jenny, 125
grooming Bostons
    anal sac care, 55–56
    coat and skin care, 53–55
    dental care, 56–57
    ear care, 58–60

    eye care, 60–61
    finding professional
       groomers, 63
    as health check, 52, 82–83
    nail care, 61–62
    supplies needed, 52

H
Hagerty spots on puppies, 20
Harding, Warren G., 15
harnesses (supplies), **30,** 31
head (physical characteristics),
    18, 20–21, **21**
health considerations. *See also*
    veterinary care
    alternative therapies, 87–88
    anal sac care, 55–56
    breed-specific problems,
       77–84
    dental care, 56
    ear care, 58–59
    eye care, 60–61
    first-aid kits, 88

    foods to avoid, 47
    general illnesses, 84–87
    grooming as health check, 52,
       82–83
    nail care, 61
    obesity and, 48–49
    parasites, 72–76
    probiotics and, 46, **46**
    for senior dogs, 88–89
    spaying/neutering, 76–77
    therapeutic food and, 43
    vaccinations and, 67–72
heartworms, 75–76
heel command, 102
hemivertebrae, 80–81
herbal remedies, 88
Herber, Gary and Sue, 125
hereditary cataracts, 81–82
hip dysplasia, 84
history of Bostons. *See* origins of
    Bostons
Hite, K. Eileen, 12
hives, 86

water consumption, 41, 85

O

obedience events, 125–127
obesity in Bostons, 48–49
O'Brien, William, 6
Orgren, Wendy, 44
origins of Bostons
    about, 6–9
    early diversity in, 9–10
    founding of BTCA, 10
    interesting facts, 15
    nickname, 6
    in Non-Sporting Group
        division, 11
    popularity of, 12
    war hero Sergeant Stubby,
        12–15
Orthopedic Foundation for
    Animals (OFA), 77–78

P

PAL/ILP number, 35, 125
parainfluenza, 68
parasites
    external, 72–74
    internal, 75–76
    in raw diets, 45
    shedding and, 54
parvovirus, 68, 71, **71**
patellar luxation (slipping
    kneecaps), 82
Perry, Vincent G., 9, 21
Pershing, John Joseph, 14
personality of Bostons, 22–24
pet-friendly lodging, 131
Pet Partners therapy program, 45
Pet Passports, 130
Petty, Gayle, 111

physical characteristics
    about, 18–19
    coat and colors, **19,** 19–21
    head, **18,** 21, **21**
    size, 19
    tail, 22
poisoning, foods to avoid, 47
positive training, 92–93, **93,** 107
postage stamps, Bostons on, 15
probiotics in diet, 46, **46**
problem behaviors
    about, 106–107
    barking, 107–108
    bitey-face activity, 24
    chewing, 109–110
    digging, 110–111
    house soiling, 111–113
    jumping up, 113–114
    nipping, 114–115
    professional help, 115
protein in diet, 39–40, 44
puppies. See also housetraining
    activities for, 127
    crate training, 94–97, **95**
    feeding considerations, 40,
        48
    gates and, 33
    Hagerty spots on, 20
    nail clipping and, 63
    problem behaviors and, 115
    socializing, 93–94
    spaying/neutering, 76–77
    swallowing pills, 83
    vaccinations, 67–72

Q

quarantine considerations, 130
quiet command, 108

R

rabies, 68, 72
Rabies Challenge Fund
    Charitable Trust, 72
rally events, 128–129
raw diet, 44–46
registering Bostons, 35
Reign Count (dog), 12
Rey, Janet V., 127
ringworm, 86–87
Rodrigue, Natacha Dagenais, 44
rotary grinders (nail care), 62

S

safety considerations
    avoiding choking, 99
    foods to avoid, 47
scabies, 73–74
scheduling feeding, 48
seal (coat and colors), 20
semi-moist food, 43
senior dogs
    health considerations, 88–89
    house soiling and, 112
Sergeant Stubby (dog), 12–15
shedding (coats and skin care),
    53–54
sit command, 93, 99–100
size (physical characteristics), 19
skin and coats. See coat and
    colors
Skyfall's Sweet Sonic Boom
    (dog), 127
slipping kneecaps (patellar
    luxation), 82
socialization and Bostons, 93–
    94, 106–107
spaying/neutering, 76–77, 112
sports and activities. See
    activities with Bostons
S.T.A.R. PUPPY program (AKC),

PHOTO CREDITS

Bonita R. Cheshier (Shutterstock.com): 120

design56 (Shutterstock.com): 112

Paul Cowan (Shutterstock.com): 85

Gary Boisvert (Shutterstock.com): 80, 107

Denis Dore (Shutterstock.com): 139

filmfoto (Shutterstock.com): 64

Brad Gibbons (Shutterstock.com): 8

Hannamariah (Shutterstock.com): 70, 138, 141

Skylar Hensley: 55, 99, 104

David Huntley (Shutterstock.com): 36 (bowl)

Misti Hymas (Shutterstock.com): 23, 33, 63

imagesbycat (Shutterstock.com): 61, 90

In-Finity (Shutterstock.com): 32

Eric Isselée (Shutterstock.com): 137

Tasha Karidis (Shutterstock.com): 82, 126

Dmitry Kramar (Shutterstock.com): 62

John Kropewnicki (Shutterstock.com): 15

kuma (Shutterstock.com): 46

LesPalenik (Shutterstock.com): 48

Shane Wilson Link (Shutterstock.com): 73

Joseph Manning: 41, 97, 98, 101

R. Gino Santa Maria (Shutterstock.com): 49

MISHELLA (Shutterstock.com): 26

Quicksnap Photo (Shutterstock.com): 25

D&D Photos (Shutterstock.com): 12, 71

Ron Rowan Photography (Shutterstock.com): 77

Stacy Price: 7, 16, 18, 28, 34, 89

Christopher T. Reggio: 110

Annette Shaff (Shutterstock.com): front cover, back cover, 1, 3, 36 (dog), 94, 116, 128

shot2design (Shutterstock.com): 84

Bob Spencer: 10, 13, 24, 30, 38, 39, 92, 106, 130

April Turner (Shutterstock.com): 42

Suzanne Maxine Uzoff: 9, 19, 40, 44, 50, 60, 66, 75, 78, 102, 114, 118, 119

Quayside (Shutterstock.com): 87

Shutterstock (Shutterstock.com): 21, 67, 81, 108, 122

Stana (Shutterstock.com): 29

Connie Wade (Shutterstock.com): 11

All other photos courtesy of Isabelle Francais and TFH archives.

ACKNOWLEDGMENTS

The author would like to express her appreciation to the following contributors: Cyndi Bussey, Sandy Cornell, Kelly Feickert, Sue Herber, Tamara Hough, Terry Jenkins, Katherine L. Kosicki, Donna Maier, Betty Ann Manganello, Jill Moore, Barbara Naas, Peggy O'Brien, Jill Ritchey, Kim Rouse, Terry Tate, Linda Trader, Suzanne Maxine Uzoff, Denice Van Driesen, and Gwenn Weyandt.

A special thank you to members of *Woof! A Boston Terrier Board*, a community of fanciers dedicated to the well-being of the breed known as the American Gentleman.

ABOUT THE AUTHOR

Patricia F. Lehman is a freelance writer specializing in the topic of dogs and their care. Her work has appeared in a variety of canine magazines, newspapers, and newsletters. She is a member and former treasurer of the Dog Writers Association of America (DWAA) and the Dog Writers Educational Trust. Her books include *The Miniature Pinscher: King of Toys, Cairn Terriers (A Complete Pet Owner's Manual)*, and *Your Healthy Puppy. King of Toys* received an Award of Excellence from the DWAA and was a finalist in the National Indie Excellence, USA Book News, and International Book Awards competitions. *Cairn Terriers* won DWAA's Maxwell Award (named in honor of veteran dog writer Maxwell Riddle) in the Best Short Book category. She has also won the Iams Company's Eukanuba Nutrition Award for the best article on canine nutrition, as well as DWAA Honorable Mention certificates for excellence in dog writing. She holds the designation Small Animal Dietitian from Hill's Pet Products. A graduate of the University of Delaware, the author lives with her family in Wilmington, Delaware.

ABOUT ANIMAL PLANET™

Animal Planet™ is the only television network dedicated exclusively to the connection between humans and animals. The network brings people of all ages together by tapping into our fundamental fascination with animals through an array of fresh programming that includes humor, competition, drama, and spectacle from the animal kingdom.

ABOUT *DOGS 101*

The most comprehensive—and most endearing—dog encyclopedia on television, *DOGS 101* spotlights the adorable, the feisty and the unexpected. A wide-ranging rundown of everyone's favorite dog breeds—from the Dalmatian to Xoloitzcuintli—this series surveys a variety of breeds for their behavioral quirks, genetic history, most famous examples and wildest trivia. Learn which dogs are best for urban living and which would be the best fit for your family. Using a mix of animal experts, pop-culture footage and stylized dog photography, *DOGS 101* is an unprecedented look at man's best friend.

At Animal Planet, we're committed to providing quality products designed to help your pets live long, healthy, and happy lives.